The Real
Bluebeard

The Real Bluebeard

JEAN BENEDETTI

DORSET PRESS
New York

This edition published by Dorset Press,
a division of Marboro Books Corporation,
by arrangement with
Stein & Day/Publishers.
1988 Dorset Press

ISBN 0-88029-245-8
(formerly ISBN 0-8128-1450-9)

Printed in the United States of America

M 9 8 7 6 5 4 3 2 1

Contents

Maps

Sources and Acknowledgements

Any new book on the life of Gilles de Rais is, of necessity, a study in interpretation. It is doubtful now whether any fresh documentary evidence will be discovered. Rather than burden the text with a multitude of footnotes, many of which will refer to works long out of print, I have chosen to indicate the sources I have relied on at the outset.

All biographers of Gilles de Rais are indebted to two main works, the Abbé Bossard's book *Gilles de Rais Maréchal de France dit Barbe Bleue, 1404–1440* (Paris 1886) and the Abbé Bourdeaut's short volume *Chantocé Gilles de Raiz et les ducs de Bretagne* (Rennes 1924). In more recent years Georges Bataille has made an invaluable contribution by establishing a detailed chronology of events and also by providing a modern French translation of the Latin account of the trial. Apart from disagreements over detail, it is Monsieur Bataille's chronology which I have accepted.

The bulk of the relevant documents concerning Gilles de Rais' life were gathered by the Abbé Bossard in the Appendices of his book. Unfortunately he did not feel able to publish the more explicit passages concerning Gilles' sexual deviations even in Latin, so that the trial record is incomplete. For the full text one must turn either to the facsimile edition published by the École de Chartes (Volume XXIII, 1862) or to the modern translation in Georges Bataille's book *Le Procès de Gilles de Rais* (Paris 1965). The full text of the *Mémoire des Héritiers,* a list of complaints concerning Gilles' extravagance drawn up by his family some years after his death when they were trying to recover the lands that had been confiscated, may also be found in Dom H. Morice's *Mémoires.*

Other important details on Gilles de Rais' life are to be found in the Abbé Bourdeaut's book, which was published after a thorough examination of local archives.

Details of Georges de la Trémoille's rise to power and his struggle with Arthur de Richemont are taken from E. Cosneau's book *Le connetable de Richemont* (Paris 1886).

The account of the siege of Orléans and the subsequent campaign in the Loire valley is based on the Chronicles collected by Quicherat in Volume IV of his work on the Trial of Joan of Arc. The larger part of the description is taken from the *Journal du siège d'Orléans* but further details have been taken from other accounts included in the same volume. Occasional use was made of the Orléans manuscript (Folio Society 1956). The terms of Gilles de Rais' agreement with La Trémoille are to be found in the history of the La Trémoille family.

The full text of the 'Mistère du Siège d'Orléans', edited by Guessard and de Certain, was published in 1862. For the material relating to the general background of the period the reader is referred to Marcellin Defourneaux's book *La vie quotidienne au temps de Jeanne d'Arc* (Hachette 1952) and to Huizinga's book *The Decline of the Middle Ages*.

Jean de Bueil's *Le Jouvencel* has also proved a useful source. This 'novel' comprises a highly self-congratulatory autobiographical account of events in the author's life. The characters in it have been given pseudonyms but are identifiable.

The quotation on page 13 is a stage direction from Bernard Shaw's *Saint Joan* and has been reproduced by permission of the Society of Authors on behalf of the Bernard Shaw Estate. The quotations on page 43 are from Robert Graves's translation of *The Twelve Caesars* by Suetonius, and are included by permission of the translator.

I would like to acknowledge the help given me by Monsieur Jean-Yves Ribault of the Archives Départementales du Cher, in Bourges, who made available his expert advice and knowledge of the period and drew my attention to certain important details. I would also like to thank Dr Ian Grimble for giving up so much of his valuable time to discuss this project with me and for allowing me to make use of the script of his Third Programme broadcast on the trial of Joan of Arc. It is to be hoped that his findings on Joan's involvement with the Witch

Cult will soon find a wider public. Finally I would like to thank Mark Barty-King for his advice and sympathetic understanding at all times.

Jean Benedetti
July 1971

The Real
Bluebeard

Gilles de Rais (Raies or Retz, 1404–1440) was reputed to have murdered ritually between 140 and 200 kidnapped children. The best estimates put the total at about sixty. He was hanged and burned at Nantes, France on 25 October 1440.

Guinness Book of Records

Allied through my mother with all the grandeur in the king-dom, and connected through my father with all that was most distinguished in Languedoc ... as soon as I could think I concluded that nature and fortune had joined hands to heap their gifts on me. This I thought because people were stupid enough to tell me so, and that idiotic presumption made me haughty, domineering and ill-tempered. I thought everything should give way before me, that the entire universe should serve my whims, and that I merely needed to want something, to be able to have it.

Marquis de Sade, *Aline and Valcour*

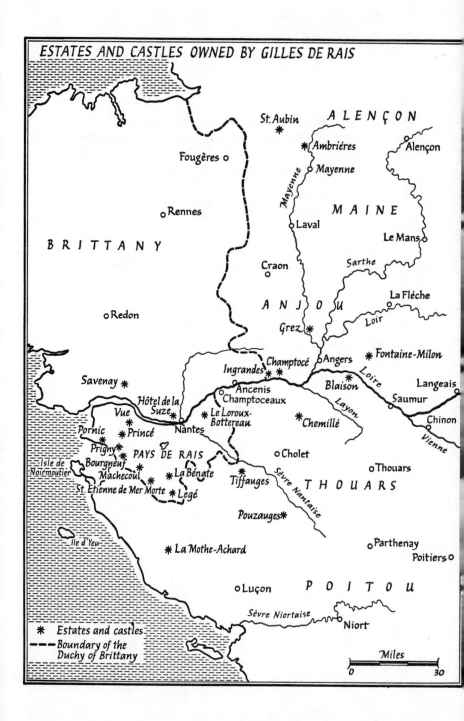

ESTATES AND CASTLES OWNED BY GILLES DE RAIS

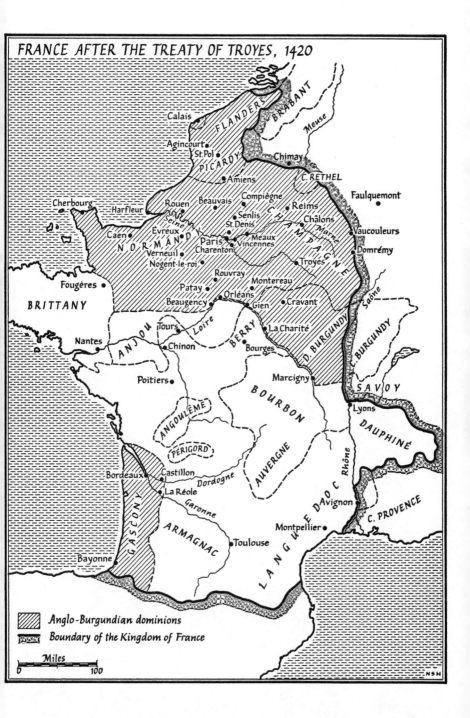

FRANCE AFTER THE TREATY OF TROYES, 1420

FLANDERS

BRABANT

Meuse

Calais

Agincourt
St.Pol

Chimay

C. RETHEL

PICARDY

Amiens

Faulquemont

Cherbourg

Harfleur

Rouen
Beauvais

Compiègne

Reims

Châlons

Vaucouleurs

Seine

Senlis

Evreux

St.Denis

Meaux

Vincennes

C H A M P A G N E

Marne

Caen

N O R M A N D Y

Paris

Charenton

Verneuil

Nogent-le-roi

Troyes

Domrémy

Fougères

Rouvray

Montereau

Saône

Patay

Orléans

Cravant

BRITTANY

Beaugency

Gien

D. BURGUNDY

C. BURGUNDY

Nantes

A N J O U

Tours

Loire

B E R R Y

La Charité

SAVOY

Chinon

Bourges

Poitiers

Marcigny

Lyons

B O U R B O N

DAUPHINÉ

ANGOULÊME

AUVERGNE

PÉRIGORD

Rhône

Castillon

Bordeaux

Dordogne

Avignon

C. PROVENCE

La Réole

Garonne

Montpellier

G A S C O N Y

L A N G U E D O C

ARMAGNAC

Toulouse

Bayonne

▨ Anglo-Burgundian dominions

▨ Boundary of the Kingdom of France

Miles

0   100

NSH

Introduction

Gilles de Rais, a young man of twenty-five, very smart and
self-possessed, and sporting the extravagance of a little curled
beard dyed blue at a clean-shaven court, comes in. He is
determined to make himself agreeable but lacks natural joy-
ousness. In fact when he defies the church some eleven years
later he is accused of trying to extract pleasure from some
horrible cruelties, and hanged. So far, however, there is no
shadow of the gallows on him. He advances gaily to the
Archbishop.

This is Shaw's description of Gilles de Rais in *Saint Joan*.
Thereafter he is indicated in the script as Bluebeard.

It is a tribute to the genius of a great writer that his insight
into the fundamental unhappiness of Gilles' character is correct,
but for the rest he is quite wrong. Gilles de Rais never had a
blue beard and was never known in his own time by that name.
If he had a beard at all it was probably red.

The error is not specifically Shaw's. He was following a long
tradition. Gilles had become Bluebeard by the time Perrault
came to write his elegant Fairy Tales in the seventeenth century.
There he could be found side by side with Cinderella and Little
Red Riding Hood. A strange juxtaposition.

Anyone might be forgiven for placing Gilles in a fairy-tale
setting. His time saw the 'cloud-capp'd towers' and 'gorgeous
palaces' being built along the Loire; clothes achieved an
undreamed-of magnificence and extravagance. The miniatures
painted for Jean de Berry show a paradise on earth where
everything, in Baudelaire's words, is 'luxury, peace and sensuous
delight'. Summers had never been so hot, the sky had never been
so blue, and even the winter snow was gentle. It was all, of

course, a lie. Beneath the enamel and gilt, French society was almost totally corrupt.

Gilles' life is intimately bound up with the life and politics of his times. Nothing could be more misleading than to regard him as some kind of monster, thrown up by nature but existing, essentially, outside the order of things. It is important, at the outset, to emphasise how typical he was of his period, how representative of his contemporaries. And so, before examining him as an active personality, as an agent, it may prove useful to consider him in his passive aspect, as a recipient, acted upon by his environment. We can then determine what modes of behaviour were available to him. He absorbed what his society had to offer, reproduced it and refracted it through his own personality and temperament. When his society finally condemned him it was not from any genuine sense of moral outrage but, as we shall see, for the most hypocritical and cynical reasons. His society never ceased to regard him as one of its own.

*   *   *   *

The Middle Ages were drawing to a close and the process of dissolution, and disillusion, had begun. Central government in France had collapsed, the law could not be enforced. Unity, such as it was, had been achieved after a long and painful struggle. Now, under the impact of the Hundred Years War, the country was splitting once more into semi-independent princedoms. The Dukes of Burgundy went their own way, negotiating with the English when it suited them; Brittany had never been part of France and treated with both English and French according to expediency. Other great nobles, like Jean de Berry, the king's uncle, lived on their estates and pursued their own interests. Worst of all, a madman was on the throne. Forty-three times Charles VI emerged from his insanity; forty-three times he relapsed into it again.

His condition unleashed a power struggle so intense that France, in addition to fighting the English, was in a virtual state of civil war. The King's uncle, Jean sans Peur, Duke of Burgundy, and his brother Louis d'Orléans fought for control of the government, alternately occupying and evacuating Paris.

When Louis d'Orléans was assassinated in 1407, at the instigation of his rival, the struggle reached its peak.

Inevitably it was France and the French people who suffered. The countryside was laid waste, arable land became overgrown with weeds, the forests crept forward once more and the towns were depopulated by the combined effects of famine, pestilence and war. The Black Death, which swept across Europe in the mid-fourteenth century, had killed off almost one-third of the population.

Time and time again attempts had been made to reconstruct the economy, and each time fresh devastation wiped out any gains. When there was a lull in hostilities armies broke up into small marauding bands, pillaging and living off the land, stealing what little was left. The distinction between soldier and brigand, tenuous at the best of times, simply did not exist. War is at root a kind of organised criminality, and heroes, frequently, psychopaths whose condition is suddenly found, in moments of crisis, to be useful. Nowhere was this more evident than in the Hundred Years War and among the military commanders on both sides.

The true nature of the Hundred Years War has frequently been obscured by later writings. It has become a rich source of many patriotic myths, on both sides of the Channel; it has become the fairy-tale world of hero-kings, like Henry V, and warrior-saints like Joan of Arc; it has, above all, been interpreted as a war of national liberation, so that Joan appears as the herald of the doctrine of self-determination, which is a later concept. (General de Gaulle set his seal on this myth, as on so many others, when he took the cross of Lorraine as the symbol of French resistance during the Second World War.) A closer study of actual events reveals a different picture. The Hundred Years War was a squabble between feudal barons, conducted on a massive scale, a fight for lands and possessions, with every man for himself, much nearer to the American West and the gang-wars of Chicago than to the idealised version of the history books. The class of warrior-nobles, of which Gilles was to become a member, fought to hold on to their possessions, and pursued their own private war-games to the detriment of their country and its populace. Indeed the English and French nobility were so closely intermarried and interconnected that it is hardly possible to talk of the two sides in terms of nationality at all.

La Hire, one of the most important captains in the final stages of the war, is an excellent example of the difference between reality and reputation. He has acquired a certain glamour through his association with Joan of Arc, with a Joan herself glamorised and distorted in accordance with later historical requirements. La Hire was a good, that is to say efficient, soldier; George Bernard Shaw presents him as a blunt honest war-dog, kept under control by Joan's saintly qualities. But for his contemporaries 'he was the most evil, the most tyrannical, the least merciful of all the captains...and because of his wickedness was called La Hire [Anger]'.*

His 'wickedness' was typical of his time. A contemporary chronicle contains an anecdote which serves to illuminate his conduct and that of his fellow soldiers. On his way to relieve the town of Montargis in September 1427, La Hire met a priest and requested absolution. The priest, naturally enough, asked him to make confession. La Hire answered that there was no time for such niceties and that he had done no more than soldiers normally do when campaigning. The priest accepted this and gave him absolution. La Hire is then said to have ended with this prayer: 'O God, I pray Thou wilt do today for La Hire what Thou wouldst have La Hire do for Thee, if he were God and Thou wert he.' The interesting feature of this story, true or not, is the shorthand which La Hire and his confessor were able to exchange. They both knew what La Hire meant when he said that he had done no more 'than soldiers normally do'.

What this implied we learn from another cleric, the Archbishop of Reims. Apart from killing their enemies, soldiers ravaged the surrounding villages and countryside, turning on their fellow countrymen with no less ferocity than on the English:

> They took women and children, without difference of age or sex, raping the women and girls; they killed the husbands and fathers in the presence of their wives and daughters; they took nurses and left the children behind so that they

* *Journal d'un Bourgeois de Paris.*

died for want of food; they took pregnant women and chained them so that they gave birth in their chains; the children were allowed to die without baptism and mother and child were thrown into the river; they took priests and monks and members of the clergy, ploughmen, chained them up in various ways and in this tortured state beat them so that certain among them were maimed for life and others driven out of their minds.... Some they roasted alive, others had their teeth ripped out, others were beaten with huge sticks, none were freed until they had given far more money than they could really afford.

The object of warfare was wealth and booty, not patriotic services, and this was the pattern of behaviour which anyone born into the nobility would be expected to accept as normal.

The chaos in the temporal world was matched by an equal disorder in the spiritual world. The Papacy was split; two rival Popes claimed the throne of Saint Peter, one sitting in Rome, the other in Avignon, each backed by rival European powers. A solution was sought and compromise candidates selected, resulting, at one moment, in there being three Popes; but the question was still not resolved. Under such circumstances there could be no question of authority, spiritual or otherwise. Those clerics who were both intelligent and well connected made a political and diplomatic career for themselves. Those who were merely well bred contented themselves with piling up benefices, which they never visited, in an attempt to combat rising costs and the inflation which was rampant over the whole of Western Europe. Money values fluctuated wildly from day to day. Many of the lower clergy lived openly with their mistresses and children. The lecherous priest became a stock figure of satirical literature and drama. It was the age of Chaucer's 'shitten shepherd'.

Religious art reflected the general malaise, the loss of confidence. It no longer showed the positive aspects of Christianity: the promise of redemption, the ascent of the soul to heaven, the hope of resurrection. Under the double influence of war and the Black Death it became obsessed with corruption and decay. Its concern was no longer the joys of paradise but the worm that devoured the corpse. The darkness of life and the darkness of death blotted out everything else. Interest in magic and witchcraft underwent one of its periodical revivals. Cult practices were never very far below the surface and emerged at moments of stress and confusion. Louis d'Orléans even summoned two members of the witch cult to court in the hope that they might succeed in curing his brother's madness where orthodox medicine and prayers had failed. They too failed.

It was natural enough for people to turn to magic. The first half of the fifteenth century was still a period of pre-scientific thinking, indeed of magical thinking, a world not merely of spells and incantations, flying broomsticks, and sexual orgies in the woods at dead of night, but one with a profound, coherent view of nature and language, the World and the Word locked in a formal pattern which is entirely alien to us.

The world was a book, a piece of prose, to be read and interpreted and if possible controlled through correct reading and judicious choice of language. The prose of the world involved everything that came into the field of knowledge—both real and mythical animals, natural phenomena and the writings of the Ancients. Fact, legend, superstition and exact observation all formed part of the pattern. Words were believed to contain the essence of things; they had power, magical power, and by controlling words it was possible to control the things they designated. Hence, to understand the grammar of the world was to achieve absolute mastery over nature. The dream of all scholars was to discover the basic language, the primal tongue, the 'Ur-text' of the universe, and thus achieve power. This activity was of course frowned on by the Church, but the Church itself shared the same basic assumptions, for prayer essentially operates on the same principle; by finding the right form of supplication it is hoped to call forth a favourable response from the Deity. The search for the primal language had its counterpart in the search for the philosopher's stone, which would transmute base metals into gold.

The problem was the degenerate state of language, which as a result of the Fall was no longer exactly conterminous with nature; words stood rather to the side of the objects they named. Rather as the months of the zodiac arranged in a circle do not coincide with the calendar months arranged in a similar concentric circle, so language no longer coincided with the world. Fortunately, all the parts of nature mirrored themselves, so some approximation was possible. Learning was therefore conceived of in terms of simile, analogy and affinity, and these mirror images could be endlessly multiplied until the approximations matched so perfectly that they became one with reality.* In all these comparisons scholars had one guiding principle, the similarity of the macrocosm, the total universe, with the microcosm, the 'little world of man'. Hence, in much pre-scientific prose, the constant employment of the human body as an analogy for the universe, or other complex organisations; the church is the body of Christ, the state is composed of various members.

The magical quest for the prime language, like the search for the philosopher's stone, proved fruitless and frustrating. Practitioners could always hear of success elsewhere but they never experienced it. Lives were spent in endless hit-and-miss attempts, ending in nothing. There seemed to be no hope anywhere, either in heaven, on earth or in hell.

*　　*　　*　　*

In this crisis only one group could have brought any kind of remedy, the nobility and the princes of the Church, but instead of applying themselves to the urgent tasks in hand they took flight in fantasy. The more brutal the facts proved, the more they lived in illusion; the more their ideas and institutions were shown to be faulty, the more they turned them into elaborate myths and surrounded them with ceremony. They lived in a world of *spectacle*, which ran parallel to the real world but glossed over all its faults. Everything there, indeed, was 'luxury, peace and sensual delight'.

The French nobility had arisen as a military caste whose express task was the defence of the population. They had posited their highest ideal in the orders of chivalry. To defend the Church, fight against untruth, protect the poor and maintain peace, those were the duties of a knight as defined by John of Salisbury in the twelfth century.

By the beginning of the fifteenth century these aims had become a mockery; the poor were subjected to the vilest atrocities, the Church was divided against itself; lying, cheating

* Michel Foucault. *Les mots et les choses* (Gallimard).

and conniving were the normal modes of conduct, and war a permanent condition. Knighthood had become a self-regarding exercise, a narcissistic concern with honour and the privileges of rank. It had no practical use. Had the French nobility been effective as a military force they might have been able to justify their conduct at other levels, but the English army had continually proved its superiority in the field, mainly through the use of simple foot-soldiers and archers. To the French aristocracy it seemed inconceivable that they should be defeated by the lower orders when they themselves wore the full panoply of knighthood and followed the rules. The simple answer would have been to change the rules and win. But they could not. To do so would have been to recognise the sham they were living, and this they were not prepared to do. Better to die, which they did. A knight would not turn aside when confronted by peasant soldiers, he preferred to ride on and be killed; he would never retreat more than forty or fifty yards, but would stand his ground and be slaughtered for his pains, or his vanity. Honourable defeat was a situation the French nobility were used to and they turned it into a virtue. Far indeed from changing the rules, they made them more elaborate still. They paid the price at Agincourt in 1415, repeating the same tactical errors that had cost them their defeat at Crécy in 1346, and showing the same indiscipline, the same obsession with individual glory, the same inability to create a coherent strategy.

However, if one could not succeed in the realities of war, there were always the tournaments. The fourteenth and fifteenth centuries witnessed an enormous elaboration of these entertainments. But the virility was gone: knights no longer clashed in mortal combat; they performed a dance, a ballet in which no-one got hurt. Certain areas of the body were designated to be struck and these were heavily padded. The victor was not the man who showed the most strength and vigour but the one who delivered his blows with the most *grace* and according to the rules. And the knights were very well dressed.

The true aims of knighthood were pushed further and further towards sport. It became fashionable to issue a general challenge with certain fantastical conditions attached. In 1415 Jean de Bourbon issued a challenge, stating that he and his knights would wear a prisoner's manacle on their left legs (gold for the knights, silver for the squires) for every Sunday for two years unless they could find a group of knights willing to take up their challenge. This was to be done in the hope of acquiring 'good renown, and the grace of the beauteous lady whose servant we are'.

The 'beauteous lady' was an essential adornment in the game of knighthood; she was a de-realised, desexualised being, whose main attribute was that she was untouchable. The cult of Woman, chaste and pure, grew side by side with the cult of the Virgin Mary, and was encouraged by the Church. It culminated in the establishment of Courts of Love where Woman was celebrated in verse and song. Significantly no flesh-and-blood female was allowed to disturb the proceedings by her actual presence; it was a strictly male affair.

It was hardly surprising that abstract Woman should be idealised in a society where actual women, or *ladies* at least, were assigned a purely property-carrying, child-bearing function. The great noble families of France were placed at the centre of the social structure and of the economy. In scope and power they can only be compared to the giant corporations of today. Within the family orbit they could count on men of ability to protect their interests: an uncle or a cousin who was a bishop or a captain, a minister or a royal favourite, and who could always be called on, through the ties of blood, to render a necessary service. Their principal object was to increase their wealth, or, at the very least, to conserve what they had already against marauders, other barons, or ambitious merchants with social pretensions. Their wealth was not abstract, not stocks and shares, equities, or quotations on the back of a newspaper; it was tangible: castles, forests, serfs, land. It could be seen, touched, flogged, ridden across.

Under such circumstances marriages were mergers, takeovers, a fusion of economic interests. When two people married it was their fortunes rather than their hearts that were joined, and their coupling was a way of transmitting still greater wealth through the succeeding generation. This is not to say that affectionate marriages did not exist, or that happiness was not often achieved, but love was not a necessary part of the transaction. If one was given a tolerable husband or wife, that was so much good luck.

As a compensation for this harsh reality the world of Romance existed. A noble lady's virtue could not be called into question; the legitimacy of her offspring was of paramount importance. Erotic drives had to be channelled towards the Ideal.

It was a pleasant idea, but bore as little relation to the facts as chivalric games bore to the realities of war. In his novel *Petit Jehan de Saintré* Antoine de la Sale gives us both a documentary and a satirical account of the education of a young knight by his lady, La Damme des Belles Cousines. He submits, obeying the convention of the times, to his mistress's commands. It is her task to school him in courtesy and manners. At her behest he travels the length and breadth of Europe in knightly service and wins great renown. He returns to lay his honours at his mistress's feet only to find he is coldly received. He discovers that his inviolate lady is bestowing her favours in all too carnal a form on a fat middle-aged Abbé. To make matters worse, Petit Jehan is soundly defeated in a bout of fisticuffs by the Abbé, who is quite happy to ignore the rules of knightly conduct and win—the experience of the French army is repeated in fictional form. To be sure Petit Jehan gets his revenge by defeating his rival in a properly arranged tournament, but this is poor compensation. The dream has proved hollow, hollow in literature, hollow in life.

The tradition of courtly love prevented no-one from taking their pleasures where they could get them. The Queen of France, Isabeau de Bavière, was the living example. She had the morals of an alley-cat and such was her notoriety that when she proclaimed her son, the future Charles VII, a bastard, few people had difficulty in believing her.

As though to block out the misery and devastation that surrounded them, the nobility transformed their forbidding mediaeval fortresses into palaces, or built afresh. They filled them with pictures, tapestries, precious objects, books, illuminated manuscripts. They became patrons and collectors. Music, both religious and secular, played an enormous part in their lives. They had their own choirs whom they dressed in lavish vestments. Their own clothes sometimes had songs embroidered in jewels on their sleeves. Few periods in the history of costume have been so extravagant. Materials were costly, designs extreme. Women's head-dresses became so tall that doorways had to be altered to accommodate them. Jewelled belts were fashionable.

One, in the royal collection, was made of solid gold and decorated with pearls, emeralds and rubies; another was made of silk and had St John's gospel embroidered on it. Shoes were pointed, the points sometimes two feet long and attached by strings to the waist to enable the wearer to walk. This fashion even pervaded armour; knights who were unhorsed in battle found that they were hindered not only by the weight they were carrying but also by their shoes, which were impossible to walk in. Thus the absurdities of fashion were added to the futility of their tactics.

Each castle was a little kingdom; it had its private army, its clerics, its entertainers, its servants. Jean de Berry, who had a reputation for meanness except where the arts were concerned, had two hundred servants to attend to his wants. While the population starved, entertainment was offered on a prodigious scale; vast meals were given, and guests showered with presents. Social life was competitive, and as the rich bourgeois increasingly provided lavish hospitality, so the nobility felt obliged to outdo them. All those who had managed to survive the depredations of war with their fortunes intact, indulged themselves in every available luxury while they listened to the *Chronicles* of Froissart and heard how brave, how noble they were, how full of chivalry and honour. French society was like a man who, finding the world inimical, retires to a gilded chamber to masturbate.

This was the world into which Gilles de Rais was born. These were the values which he was offered and which he accepted. Almost every feature of life discussed here will be found in the course of his career, writ large and then larger still. The difference between Gilles and his contemporaries was one of *scale*. In an age of extravagance he was super-extravagant; in an age of crime he was a super-criminal.

Part One
GLORY

I

Birth of an Heir

GILLES DE RAIS was born as a result of a legal wrangle affecting property. To understand the precise nature of the dispute and thus of his coming into the world we must consult his family tree. This will enable us to understand the complicated system of relationships and inheritances which caused his parents to marry.

Both Guy de Laval, his father, and Marie de Craon, his mother, were members of the same clan. They were distant relatives, sufficiently distant for there to be no impediment to their union in canon or civil law. Their marriage resulted in their combined wealth being kept within the confines of the family, a consideration of the highest importance.

Events were set in motion in 1400 by Jeanne Chabot, known as Jeanne la Sage, to distinguish her from her kinswoman Jeanne la Folle, whose madness consisted in no more than marrying a man her family disapproved of. Jeanne la Sage was the last of the Rais family. She was separated from her husband, had no children and no close relatives. Her brother Girard Chabot had died childless in 1351. The Rais titles and lands were hers to bequeath—but who was to inherit?

The problem was urgent, not only because of her advanced age but because her lands were in danger of being appropriated by the Duke of Brittany. Jean IV kept up a continual campaign against her. He was particularly anxious to get possession of her castles which were strategically placed along his border and provided a bulwark against the King of France.

As a preliminary measure Jeanne Chabot placed herself under the protection of the *Parlement* of Paris. She then began to look for an heir. In point of fact she had one already, her second cousin Guy de Laval, grandson of Guy IX de Laval and

Jeanne la Folle. He was a man well able to look after his own.

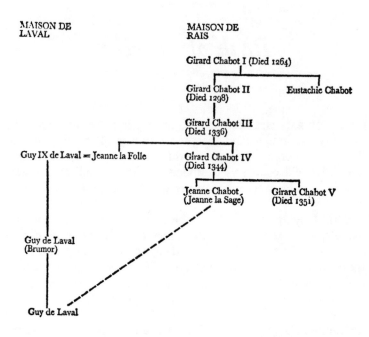

MAISON DE
LAVAL

MAISON DE
RAIS

Girard Chabot I (Died 1264)

Girard Chabot II
(Died 1298)　　　　　Eustachie Chabot

Girard Chabot III
(Died 1336)

Guy IX de Laval = Jeanne la Folle　　Girard Chabot IV
(Died 1344)

Jeanne Chabot　　Girard Chabot V
(Jeanne la Sage)　(Died 1351)

Guy de Laval
(Brumor)

Guy de Laval

Unfortunately there was a serious impediment. After the death of her husband Jeanne la Folle had made an unsuitable second marriage with Jean de la Musse-Pont Hüe, a *mésalliance* as far as the rest of the family were concerned. As a result she and her descendants were disinherited in perpetuity from the Rais estates and titles. A special legal dispensation would be necessary to restore Guy de Laval's rights.

Jeanne Chabot was willing to make such a dispensation, set aside the act of disinheritance and adopt Guy de Laval as her heir on one condition: that he should take the style 'de Rais'. Guy de Laval was hardly the man to allow a name to stand between himself and a vast fortune. Accordingly, on 23 September 1401, he signed an agreement adopting the new name. From 1 January 1402 he was known as Guy de Rais. The inheritance was his.

But then, having gone to so much trouble, Jeanne Chabot changed her mind. The precise reason for this is not known, but she altered her will, disinherited Guy de Laval and bequeathed her fortune to her only other relative, more distant still, Catherine de Machecoul, to whom she was connected on the female side. Catherine de Machecoul was a widow with one son, Jean de Craon.

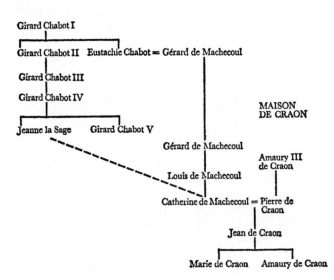

It is possible that Jean de Craon, rapacious and avaricious as he was, and knowing that the Rais fortunes were for the taking, made a direct approach to the old woman, pointing out that his mother Catherine was also a relative, that he was her sole heir, and had a son Amaury who was young and vigorous, as well as a daughter. If his family were made the beneficiaries of her will the Rais succession was already assured. After all Guy de Laval had as yet no children. Perhaps he never would have. At all events, whether persuaded by these arguments or not, Jeanne Chabot changed her mind and set off a chain of events which was to culminate in the birth of Gilles de Rais.

Guy de Laval had no intention of seeing a fortune snatched

away from his family a second time. He sued, demanding that his original agreement with Jeanne la Sage should be upheld. He had kept his side of the bargain, changed his name and in so doing made his expectations public. Jean de Craon, naturally, defended the suit. It was submitted to the Parlement of Paris and vigorously argued on both sides. Mediaeval law was not a swift process at the best of times and this case was an embarrassment to all concerned. No-one wished to offend either of these two powerful families. With delaying tactics the case could have been dragged out interminably. It lasted for a year at least, as can be seen from part of a statement submitted by Jean de Craon in 1403. A compromise was needed badly. Fortunately for all concerned one was readily available.

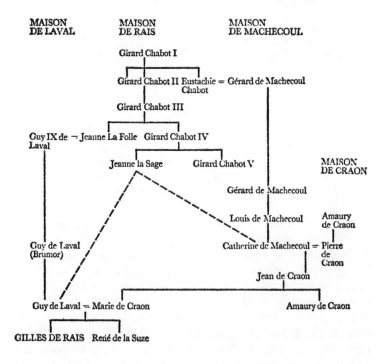

Jean de Craon was greedy and unscrupulous but he was also an expert accommodator and diplomat. He proposed that Marie

de Craon, his daughter, should marry Guy de Laval, thus unit-
ing the interests of both families. He then set up a complicated
series of interlocked legacies designed to satisfy everyone
concerned. Jeanne la Sage's will in favour of Catherine de
Machecoul was to stand. She would then make a will in favour
of her son, Jean de Craon, who in his turn would bequeath
all the de Rais estates to his daughter Marie. She, in her turn,
would sign them over, as part of the marriage settlement, to
her husband, Guy de Laval, who would honour his undertaking
to adopt the style de Rais. All the wealth would thus be concentrated on their issue. Jeanne la Sage was approached by both
sides in the dispute and accepted the solution, doubtless with
some relief.

The marriage of Guy de Rais and Marie de Craon was celebrated by the Abbé Jean du Bellay on 5 February 1404. No
time was lost in getting an heir and before the end of the year
a child was born in the ominously named Black Tower at the
castle of Champtocé. The succession of the Rais titles and
estates was thus settled once and for all.

The child was baptised Gilles, a name which appears nowhere
else in the family tree. From this it has been assumed that in
their anxiety to beget a son Guy de Rais and his wife made a
pilgrimage to Saint-Gilles du Cotentin, where lived a hermit
whose special gift seems to have been the granting of an heir.

The christening itself was a resplendent affair. Jean de Craon
was godfather. The local nobility and peasantry were summoned
to the castle chapel and there, lighted candles in their hands,
they witnessed the solemn initiation of Gilles de Rais into the
Catholic Church. The young mother was showered with gifts.
Sixty years after, the Abbé Auger de Bris of Saint-Georges-sur-
Loire could still recall that day and remembered that he himself
had presented Marie de Rais with a tame hare.

Jeanne Chabot died in 1406, a happy woman.

2

Childhood and Adolescence

GILLES WAS GIVEN into the charge of a wet-nurse, Guillemette la Drappière, a respectable woman of the district, who had a young son of her own. Gilles' relationship with his wet-nurse seems to have been an affectionate one. He remembered her all his life, and he also took an interest in Jean la Drappière, his *'frère de lait'*. The two boys were brought up together on the express order of Guy de Rais and received instruction from the two tutors he had appointed, Georges de Boszac, a priest with a degree in law, and Michel de Fontenay, also a priest. (Jean later became a priest, and Gilles appointed him as his personal chaplain.)

Judging by contemporary accounts of social life, it seems unlikely that Marie de Rais would have had much time to attend to her son. A great deal of care had to go into dressing and toilette. In an age when everything had to be done by hand this was a laborious time-consuming business, even with an army of servants on hand. But it was necessary : entertainments were long and lavish, visits elaborate; amusement and diversions filled many hours of the day and there was much local and court gossip to discuss. It was an unreal, trivial world in which the imperative, human demands of a baby could have little place.

Of Gilles' father the most that we can say is that he made adequate arrangements for his son's upbringing, appointing well-qualified tutors and designating a guardian when he knew that he himself was dying. Perhaps he was not an unsympathetic or ungenerous man : the fact that he agreed to Gilles and Jean being brought up together may be an indication of this. But that he had much time to spend with the boy, between his duties as a feudal lord, his social life and his long hunting trips, is doubtful.

Not that Gilles wandered around the castle a lost child, ignored and pushed aside by everyone. He was far too important for that. He received a great deal of attention—most of it, one suspects, of entirely the wrong kind.

Gilles was the little prince, the heir apparent, the biological culmination of much legal wrangling. He was the living proof that it had not all been in vain. He was the solution to everyone's problems. The investment in him was enormous on all sides; to his parents he was the future of the estate, to the servants he was a living, both now and later. He was cocooned in luxury, groomed for a brilliant future, plied with every privilege available to the first son of an aristocratic family. If he threw tantrums, who was there to correct him? A slap could result in a complaint to the boy's parents and a whipping for some unfortunate servant. Besides, the lower orders were used to the caprices of their masters. To be unreasonable even to the point of insanity was a master's privilege, and Gilles was to be a master *par excellence,* with the hopes of two, later three families bearing down on him. No other child in France, or in Europe, was endowed with such expectations.

In 1407, when Gilles was three years old, his brother René de la Suze was born. Relations between him and his brother never seem to have been very cordial, and René was not involved in any of his brother's excesses. In fact, he appears very little in the course of the story, except to complain about Gilles's extravagance and to try and get hold of his property, both during and after his life. For the most part they seem to have hated each other with quiet efficiency.

As soon as he was old enough, Gilles, pampered, aggressive and destructive, was handed over to his tutors and an instructor to be turned into a noble lord, fit to take his place in society and to perform his feudal duties. His education was divided into two distinct disciplines, military on the one hand, moral and intellectual on the other. Both would have been conducted with meticulous regard for formal procedures; militarily he had to be prepared to become an effective soldier, versed in the codes of chivalry; intellectually he had to receive the necessary instruction for the salvation of his soul and to be initiated into the study and appreciation of the classics. Both entailed a mastery of Latin, the language through which religion and culture were transmitted. He showed aptitude in all fields. Throughout his life, in fact, he showed marked ability in any activity he chose to interest himself in.

Daily he would have practised the arts of war and destruction under careful supervision until they became second nature. He was later to prove the efficacy of his training when he fought side by side with Joan of Arc during that one dramatic year when France pulled herself from her knees.

The tutors concerned with his moral and intellectual development supplied him with formulae which were to govern his thinking all his life. In doing this they merely passed on to him the learning and the modes of thought of their time.

*   *   *   *

In 1415 Gilles lost both his parents. Guy de Rais was gored by a wild boar while out hunting. His death was a slow one and he had time to draw up his will and make provision for his sons. Under the terms of Guy de Rais' will, made on 28 September 1415, Jean Tournemine de la Junaudaye was appointed 'guardian, tutor, defender, legal administrator of his sons and heirs Gilles and René and of all their wealth'.

He further stipulated that the tutors he had appointed should continue in their posts, particularly as Georges de la Boszac was a close personal friend and could be trusted.

The question of Marie de Rais' death is more problematic. Certainly no mention is made of her after 1415. Some historians maintain that her death preceded her husband's and that she was buried in the church of Notre-Dame de Rais at the Abbey of Buzay earlier in the year. However, the Abbé Bossard states quite categorically that she remarried and that her second husband was Charles d'Estouville. If this is so, her attitude to her children must have been callous in the extreme, for she never contacted Gilles again, neither in his moments of glory, nor in those of darkest tragedy. She is not mentioned in any of the legal disputes over family property; the probability is that she died before her husband.

One of the most striking features of Guy de Rais' will is the care with which Jean de Craon is excluded. Nowhere is he mentioned: nothing is asked of him, except, by implication, that he should keep out of his grandson's affairs. None the less he was the boy's nearest relative and, with his powerful connections, the obvious choice as a guardian. Why then was he excluded? Most biographers agree that by this deliberate omission Guy de Rais was expressing an opinion of his father-in-law's moral character. Everything we know of Jean de Craon suggests that he was little better than a bandit, ruthlessly dedicated to his own gain and self-interest. In an age not remarkable for what would today be classed as 'good citizenship' he distinguished himself by his lawlessness. Guy de Rais was not anxious for his two sons to be subjected to this kind of influence. However, he might have spared himself the trouble. Within a matter of months all his careful provisions were set aside.

> After the death of the said Guy de Rays [sic], father of the said Messire Gilles, this same Messire Gilles, a minor young in years, remained in the guardianship of the aforesaid Jehan de Craon, his maternal grandfather who was old, ancient and of very great age.

It is difficult to say how long a man as acquisitive as Jean de Craon would have tolerated his son-in-law's will, even under normal circumstances, and allowed himself to be tantalised by the sight of so much power and wealth just out of his reach. In the event his hand was forced.

The year 1415 was one of national disaster, as well as of personal disaster for Gilles. On October 25 the French were soundly beaten at Agincourt, described by a chronicler as 'the most disgraceful event that has ever occurred in the history of our country'. Among the dead on the battlefield, with the arrows, according to one report, firmly sticking from his back, was Jean de Craon's son and heir Amaury. With his daughter Marie dead, or so we suppose, there was no one to inherit but his grandson Gilles. The Craon fortune was thus to be added to those of the Montmorency-Laval and de Rais families.

Jean de Craon moved with customary speed and before the end of the year Gilles was in his sole charge. The guardian whom Guy de Rais had appointed, Jean Tournemine de la Junaudaye, had done what his name suggested and turned his face in another direction, away from the Rais estates.

We should not underestimate the importance of Gilles' double bereavement and the upheaval it caused in his life. He and his parents may have been kept apart to a large extent by social usage, but this does not mean to say he felt no love for them or did not need them. He was continuously aware of their presence. The hierarchical chain of authority and command so rigorously enforced by mediaeval society led inevitably to his mother and father. They were the centre of the universe; they provided his stability and security. With their deaths a whole structure disintegrated, to be replaced by two different sets of arrangements within the space of a few months. Having settled into a new routine with his guardian and tutors, he had to adjust to different circumstances with his grandfather. This implied a markedly changed way of life, free from all restraining moral influences. The effect on *any* child would have been disturbing. In Gilles' case it marks the first, but not the last occasion when the world he had known was altered with brutal suddenness.

As we have seen in the extract from his letter to the king, quoted above, when René de la Suze tried to recover the family estates which had been confiscated after his brother's death he described his grandfather as being 'old, ancient and of very great age' (*'viele, ancien et de moult grant aage'*). Presumably at this point he ran out of synonyms. The official family version was that Jean de Craon was doddering and incapable of controlling his grandson, who was already showing signs of the insanity that led him to squander his money so recklessly.

In fact Jean de Craon was under sixty when he took charge of his grandson—a good age admittedly, considering the expectation of life in that period, but hardly dotage—and in the next few years he was to show every sign of intelligence and vigour. He had all the qualities necessary for survival in this difficult period. He knew by instinct where his interest lay; he knew when and when not to make an issue of a problem, and when, in a world of rapidly changing alliances and broken promises, to change sides. He had a flair, too, for negotiation and diplomacy. His own daughter's marriage was evidence enough of that. And when talk failed he knew how to act.

Nothing is perhaps more indicative of his patterns of behaviour than his conduct during the running dog-fight which he was engaged in with the Compagnie des Marchands et Mariniers Fréquantant la Rivière de Loire. These merchants transported their goods along the waterway of the Loire to the coast. Unfortunately for them they passed through lands belonging to Jean de Craon, notably Champtocé, and were obliged to pay toll duties. These, needless to say, were excessive to the point of ruin. The merchants sued. Jean de Craon riposted by hauling them off their boats and beating them, hoping to force them to drop legal proceedings. However, they were as obstinate as he was and finally Guillaume de Villers, the king's representative, presented himself at Champtocé, accompanied by a large retinue, and informed Jean de Craon that the king had taken the merchants under his protection and that any coercion was to cease forthwith. This was in 1413 when central government in France still had some meaning. Not wishing to take issue with the king, Jean de Craon submitted.

No doubt he hoped to pass on to his grandson his political astuteness and his passion for acquiring wealth. He was to be disappointed. Gilles never had any political sense whatsoever: all his life he was manipulated and exploited by men more able than himself, and, above all, he was extravagant. None the less, Jean de Craon made every effort to initiate his grandson into regional and national politics. But this, for the moment at least, was not his prime concern.

The first move Jean de Craon made was to find a suitable wife for his grandson. As Gilles was only twelve years old it would be, of course, a purely business arrangement. The first candidate was Jeanne Paynel, who at the time was less than four years old. Her age did not matter. What did was that she was one of the richest heiresses in the whole of Normandy. What was more, her father, Foulques de Hambuic, was dead. In accordance with local custom she had been placed under the king's protection until she reached her majority. The king had entrusted her to the family of Roche-Guyon who had hit upon the convenient idea of engaging her to their own son who was all of seven years old. When Jeanne's family protested at this manoeuvre the authorities removed her from the care of the Roche-Guyons and looked for more suitable guardians.

It was at this point, the psychological moment as always, that Jean de Craon chose to intervene. The child's grandfather was Charles Dinan, Baron de Châteaubriant, a nobleman with a fine pedigree and no money. Jean de Craon persuaded him to ask for custody of the girl, promising him enough money to provide a dowry plus 4,000 *livres** in cash to settle his own debts. Without waiting for the decision of the courts regarding the child's custody, Dinan signed a marriage contract on her behalf with Jean de Craon on 14 January 1417. Unfortunately for him he was premature. The authorities had not saved the girl from one set of grasping hands to entrust her to another. She was placed in the charge of her aunt Jacqueline Paynel, and any further discussion of marriage was forbidden until she came of age. In fact she became a nun and died as Abbess of Notre-Dame de Lisieux.

Thwarted in this direction, Jean de Craon turned his attention to the neighbouring province of Brittany, where he and his grandson owned considerable estates. He asked for the hand of Béatrice de Rohan. Béatrice was considerably less wealthy than Jeanne Paynel, and her father could only offer 1,500 *livres* as a dowry, but she had the inestimable advantage of being the niece of the Duke of Brittany, whom Jean de Craon was cultivating at the time.

The marriage contract was signed at Vannes on 28 November 1418 in the presence of a crowd of notables and church dignitaries. Jean de Craon seemed to be sufficiently pleased with the arrangement to buy a house in Nantes which he proceeded to transform into the Hôtel de la Suze, as proof of his Breton sympathies. However, it did him no good. The contract was never fulfilled, although the precise reason for this is not known. It is possible the girl died.

In 1419 all questions of marriage were interrupted by a sudden crisis in regional politics. The Duke of Brittany's family, the Montforts, had been in feud with the other leading family of the province, the Penthièvres, for something like a hundred years. The quarrel was as old as the Hundred Years War itself, whose course it strongly resembled. It would lie dormant for a time and then suddenly flare up again. Its origins, as with so many feuds, were obscure and probably forgotten by the participants themselves. Traditionally the Laval and Rais families supported the Penthièvre faction, coming as they did

---

* It is difficult to provide any clear guide to French currency in the fifteenth century. Values fluctuated and a number of coins were in circulation. The main terms used in this book are the *écu*, the *réal* and the *livre tournois*.

from the southern part of Brittany; the Montforts relied on the families of the north. Besides, Bertrand du Guesclin, Gilles' great-uncle, had been a close friend, and perhaps more, of Olivier de Clisson, head of the Penthièvre family. This, however, meant nothing to Jean de Craon; tradition had to be weighed against immediate interest. In 1419, with typical acumen, he switched sides and threw in his lot and that of his grandson with Jean V de Montfort, Duke of Brittany.

The causes of this fresh outbreak of the feud were rooted in the Hundred Years War. The Dauphin, the future Charles VII, had never given up hope of mounting the throne of France despite every possible discouragement from all quarters. He was incensed at the behaviour of the Duke of Brittany who constantly promised to send him troops which never arrived. He therefore mounted a plot with Olivier de Blois, Comte de Penthièvre, who was encouraged in the matter by his mother Marguerite de Clisson. The idea was to bring the Duke and his offending province to heel.

The plot was a simple one. Olivier de Clisson was to invite the Duke to a banquet at his castle of Champtoceaux. It must have occurred to Jean V that this was a strange offer, considering that their two families were at war. Possibly he regarded it as a peace overture, possibly he imagined that they dare not lay a finger on him. He was wrong in both cases. Upon his arrival he was seized, put in chains, thrown into an insanitary dungeon and threatened with sudden death.

On 23 February 1420, the Duchess of Brittany called a meeting of the Estates General in the town of Vannes. Making a calculatedly dramatic appearance with her children, she appealed for help in rescuing her husband. Gilles was present at this meeting, with his grandfather, and it was his debut in public life. A few days previously, along with the other nobles loyal to the Montfort cause, he had sworn a solemn oath of allegiance, vowing to deliver his prince and fight to the last drop of his blood. 'We swear upon the cross to employ our bodies and our goods, and to live and die upon this quarrel.'

There is some doubt concerning the precise rôle which Gilles played in the subsequent negotiations and hostilities. The Abbé Bossard is quite convinced that he participated fully in the fighting, raising troops at his own expense and leading them into battle, and showing the first signs of the ostentation that was to distinguish him in later years. Some writers, on the other hand, have objected that his name appears nowhere in the records, and that he was a mere sixteen years old. None the less, after the Penthièvre faction had been finally routed, the Duke stated that he did not know how to show his gratitude 'for the good and loyal services of his cousins de la Suze [i.e. Jean de Craon] and de Rais', which seems to indicate some degree of participation. In any case it was not unusual for the sons of noblemen to receive their baptism of fire in their teens. Life was shorter and maturity came younger; university entrance, for instance, was at fourteen and there are many examples in Shakespeare of boys fighting side by side with their fathers. In all probability Jean de Craon, who played a prominent part in the conduct of national affairs, allowed his grandson to play a limited rôle on the periphery. What was more important for Gilles was that he made contact with men who were to influence the whole course of his life: Jean V of Brittany and his brother Arthur de Richemont, future Constable of France; Jean de Malestroit, Chancellor of Brittany and Bishop of Nantes (and his future prosecutor); and Georges de la Trémoille, a distant cousin.

For the moment things looked black for the Duchess and her unfortunate children; her husband was in a dungeon and his brother Arthur, an experienced soldier, was a prisoner of the English. At the meeting of the Estates General it was decided to create Alain de Rohan Lieutenant General of Brittany with full powers. His immediate task was to raise an army of 50,000 men. This is an enormous figure for the period and probably represents wishful thinking rather than fact. It was common practice in the Chronicles of the time to exaggerate the number of soldiers involved in any engagement and to falsify casualty lists in favour of whichever side one happened to be writing for. Everyone knew and nobody cared. But the largest army of the period, for a pitched battle such as Agincourt, rarely exceeded 7,000 men. It was further decided to send an embassy to Henry V in London to arrange for the ransom and release of Arthur de Richemont; it consisted of Guy de Laval and Jean de Craon, and it was successful.

During this time the Penthièvre family had not been idle. They ravaged the de Rais lands and estates in Brittany, Larou-

Botereau, Saint-Etienne-de-Mer-Morte and Machecoul among others. They must have felt particularly bitter towards Jean de Craon and his grandson for betraying them after a hundred years of family friendship and they expressed their feelings in the most vindictive manner. As for the unfortunate Jean V, they dragged him from castle to castle, tied to a horse, travelling through the night, hardly giving him enough food to keep him alive. They made a round trip, finally coming back once more to Champtoceaux.

However, the tide was turning against them, and their friends found it politic to withdraw their support: the army raised with great speed by Alain de Rohan was on the march. In a last desperate act of revenge they attacked the lands of Gilles de Rais and his grandfather once more and took the castle of La Mothe-Achard. In the meantime they were losing their own strongholds; Lamballe, Guingamp, Roche-Derrien, Jugon, Châteaulin and Braon fell in quick succession. Champtoceaux itself was besieged and finally fell on 15 July 1420. The Penthièvre family took to its heels. Jean V was released from his dungeon and, as a reprisal, ordered the immediate demolition of the castle he had come to hate so much.

The fighting over, there were political debts to be settled. Even before the final victory the Duchess of Brittany had granted Jean de Craon the income from the lands that had once belonged to Olivier de Blois and his accomplices. In the midst of the celebration following his release, which included a triumphal entry into Nantes and in which Gilles can be assumed to have played a glittering part, Jean V confirmed his wife's proclamation, made on July 10 at Oudun, granting them 'all the lands that the malefactors and accomplices of Olivier de Blois, formerly Count of Penthièvre, and Charles, his brother, had possessed'. This is extremely generous and indicates the importance of the rôle which Jean de Craon assumed in the struggle. And, naturally enough, any glory which·fell on him was immediately reflected on to his grandson, who had become the centre of his life and hopes.

The Breton parliament found that the Duke had been too generous and on September 21 reduced the compensation granted to Jean de Craon to 240 *livres* per annum. A week later Jean V, feeling that this was insufficient to discharge his debt, added a further 100 *livres* per annum, confiscated from Ponthus de la Tour, one of the supporters of the Penthièvre family, 'to compensate for the losses which his faithful servants had suffered by the occupation of many of their estates, among others La Mothe-Achard'. For the moment relations could not have been better between Gilles, his grandfather and the Duke of Brittany's family. The Duke was grateful for his release, his brother for being ransomed, and Jean de Craon and Gilles had been suitably rewarded. The sun shone on all of them. Everything was for the best in the best of all possible worlds.

Gilles and his grandfather returned to their castles to resume normal life. What their 'normal' life consisted of Gilles indicated in his later confessions: the unbridled satisfaction of all his whims and fancies accompanied by excessive eating and drinking at table. The pattern of their lives seems to have been a round of good living occasionally punctuated by marauding raids and sorties.

Jean de Craon had strong acquisitive instincts but he was prepared to spend within reasonable limits. He was not a Balzacian miser hoarding his gold and secretly counting it at night. He had a position to keep up, and so had his grandson as potentially the richest man in Europe. Champtocé has been described as a little court, with young Gilles sitting on the throne, pampered and fussed over by his grandfather, dressed like a king and behaving like a tyrant. Consciously or unconsciously Jean de Craon had an interest in keeping Gilles in a dependent position. The longer he remained a child the easier he would be to control. It was always Jean de Craon who planned and calculated; all Gilles had to do was enjoy the escapades and the luxury. Perhaps this was the reason why he never developed any political sense, in the widest meaning of the term. But he seems to have been happy. And if there was still occasionally a feeling of emptiness inside he had all the compensations—food, clothes, literature and bloodshed. There were clowns and minstrels, actors and jugglers to entertain him, and there were long days of hunting. Never a moment that he could not fill and forget.

The size of mediaeval meals appears staggering to us and they seem to have been a matter of survival rather than nutrition. We may get some idea of what Gilles meant when he spoke of excesses at table if we consider the following menu for a *modest* meal in a bourgeois household:

First Course
White leeks with capon: roast goose with sausages, pieces of beef and mutton, a stew of hares, veal and rabbits.
Second Course
Partridges, rabbits, plovers, dressed pigs, pheasants (for the high table only), meat, a fish jelly.
Entrements
Fish: carp.
(For the high table only): Swans, pheasants, bitterns, herons, etc.
To follow
Venison, rice with milk and saffron, capon pâté, custard flans, pastry with cream, fruit, pastries, claret.

Wine was drunk at the end of the meal. It tended to be rather sour and to deteriorate quickly. As a result it was doctored with sugar, herbs and spices to form hippocras, a powerful, heady substance that easily broke down inhibitions and ethical barriers.

For quiet relaxation Gilles could turn to the Latin authors he had been introduced to by his tutors. No complete list survives of the books he possessed. The only titles we have are those which occur in his accounts. There is however a strong tradition, which it seems reasonable to accept, that one of his favourite works was *The Twelve Caesars* of Suetonius. Certainly there are strong correspondences between the vices Suetonius describes and Gilles' own later conduct.

Gilles could, for example, read of Tiberius' playful habit of filling his guests with enormous quantities of wine and then tying a string round their genitals so that they could not urinate, or of how he executed twenty people a day. He could then pass on to Caligula:

No parallel can be found for Caligula's far-fetched extravagancies. He invented new kinds of baths and the most unnatural dishes and drinks—bathing in hot and cold perfumes, drinking valuable pearls dissolved in vinegar, and providing his guests with golden bread and meat. For several days in succession he scattered largesse from the roof of the

Julian Basilica, and built Liburnian galleys with ten banks of oars, jewelled poops, multi-coloured sails, and with huge baths, colonnades and banqueting halls aboard—not to mention growing vines and apple-trees of different varieties. . . Villas and country houses were run up for him regardless of expense—in fact Caligula seemed interested only in doing the apparently impossible . . . in less than a year he squandered Tiberius' entire fortune of 27 million gold pieces and an enormous amount of other treasure besides.

Reading on further, Gilles would learn how Nero bankrupted himself, how he had a passion for the theatre and display:

Nero never wore the same clothes twice. He seldom travelled with a train of less than 1,000 carriages; the mules were shod with silver, the muleteers wore Carnusian wool, and he was escorted by Maxacian horsemen from Morocco, and outriders with jingling bracelets and medallions.

However, Gilles' later career is not explicable in terms of imitation only. What he found in Suetonius was a confirmation of his own impulses. Here were emperors indulging their fantasies with a lavishness that even he could admire. Here, in fact, was something he could look up to with respect. His grandfather was a clever man, but he was not drawn to emulate him. But here was extravagance on a scale he could not match, although he could try. This rush towards financial ruin fascinated him as a gambler is fascinated by the prospect that he must lose. And was he not an emperor, too? At any rate he was treated like one. For the moment his grandfather controlled the purse-strings, but when he came into his own what dreams of splendour he could realise.

While Gilles was indulging in his private fantasies Jean de Craon was trying to increase his fortune still more by arranging a suitable marriage. By the end of 1420 he was in a position once more to devote all his energies to domestic matters. The feud appeared to have been decisively settled and the war was dormant. His choice lighted on Catherine de Thouars, daughter of Milet de Thouars and Béatrice de Montjean, whose estates, by a fortunate coincidence, bordered the Craon lands in the east. The question arises as to why Jean de Craon did not turn to her in the first place. She would have seemed the most obvious choice. Possibly he was discouraged by the fact that Catherine was a distant cousin. Her relationship to Gilles was only of the eighth degree but that was sufficiently close to infringe Church laws on consanguinity. However, any such considerations were set aside now that other candidates were dead or out of reach.

Not that Jean de Craon was the only one to look with greedy eyes in Catherine's direction. Her father was absent on a pilgrimage to Brabant—some authors maintain he was away fighting. The occasion had been seized by various young men to press their suit. This they did not by the normal method of sending letters swearing undying love, accompanied by presents, but by setting up camp and virtually laying siege to the castle where she lived. The unfortunate girl was virtually a prisoner. Milet de Thouars' squire, Jacques Meschin de la Roche-Aireault, who had been left in charge by his master, was a young man of enterprise and vigour, and he obliged these over-enthusiastic suitors to decamp and leave his mistress and her daughter in peace. News came shortly after that Milet de Thouars was dying of a fever at Meaux and Jacques Meschin left Tiffauges to go to him.

It was at this moment that Jean de Craon acted. On 22 November 1420, Gilles rode to Tiffauges with a party of men and kidnapped Catherine. A week later, on November 30, they were married in a remote little chapel. No banns were published and the ceremony was conducted by an obscure monk who doubtless had been terrorised into obedience. Catherine's mother was not present and, needless to say, no dispensation had been obtained from the Church regarding the couple's blood relationship. Presumably the gap between the kidnapping and the marriage was to establish the fact that they had become man and wife in fact if not in canon law. Whether they had or not we do not know; their only child was not born until 1429.

It is possible that the almost certain opposition of the Church and the presence of so many rivals may have forced Gilles and his grandfather into this course of action, but one cannot escape the thought that they would both have taken a certain vicious pleasure in the violent nature of the undertaking. For Jean de Craon it was doubtless a pre-emptive move, of a familiar pattern—grab now, negotiate later. Certainly he was not prepared to become involved in an interminable wrangle with the Church which would probably result in another suitor jumping in. As far as Gilles was concerned it must have been rather a relief. He would not have been interested in a formal courtship and marriage. He was not interested in women, they had no place in his life. Gilles never wanted Catherine, he never cared for her, he never paid her any regard. As the Abbé Bourdeaut points out, the women in the Gilles' family are all vague figures. They flit like shadows across his path. The only thing interesting about Catherine was her lands. The manner in which Gilles took her is perfectly expressive of his attitude. She was depersonalised, devalued, humiliated; treated like booty carried off on a cattle raid.

Church reaction was swift. Hardouin de Bueil, Bishop of Angers, who just happened to be a relative of the bride's mother, declared the marriage null and void on the grounds of consanguinity. Jean de Craon was not unduly perturbed. He was skilled in the diplomatic game and he knew which palms to grease. A representative was despatched to Rome to plead the cause of two young 'lovers'. In accordance with custom, Jean de Craon's representative doubtless deposited a large sum of money in the Vatican coffers.*

In the meantime Catherine's property had been seized. Béatrice de Montjean now asked Jacques Meschin, who had proved so effective in the past, to negotiate a marriage settlement with Jean de Craon. This he did, allowing Gilles to keep one-third of the Thouars estates if the marriage was allowed.

The negotiations, both ecclesiastical and civil, dragged on for two years. Finally the Pope, influenced both by the arguments of Jean de Craon's ambassador—although it must have been obvious by then that if Catherine was expecting a child the pregnancy had been long enough to verge on the miraculous—but probably more by the contribution made to Church funds, decided to allow the marriage. His letter of authorisation was dated 24 April 1422. Almost a month later, on 22 June, after a token separation, for form's sake, Gilles and Catherine were remarried by the Bishop of Angers himself at his own castle at Chalonnes, in the presence of the vicar of Champtocé, two canons from Blaizon and a large and distinguished congrega-

---

* Michel Bataille. *Gilles de Rais* (Editions Planète, 1966).

tion. The Bishop, who had taken some part in the negotiations, had also received a substantial gift of alms from Jean de Craon, no doubt as proof of repentance.

During this period Jean de Craon's wife died. He lost no time in remarrying. His new bride was Anne de Sillé, Catherine's grandmother. Doubtless this was a move to secure the Thouars estate for good and all, leaving no doubt where the legacies would go. As a corollary to this it is worth noting that Gilles's brother René married Anne de Sillé's niece Anne de Champagne.

There remained the problem of the marriage settlement which, from Jean de Craon's point of view, was far from satisfactory. The two most important castles, Tiffauges and Pouzauges, strategically placed on the borders of Poitou, were not legally his grandson's although he was in physical possession of them. The marriage contract had to be set aside and Gilles' *de facto* possession made legal.

However, Jean de Craon was not the only one to remarry. Late in 1422 Béatrice de Montjean married Jacques Meschin, who had served her so well. Two conflicting versions exist of the events leading up to their union and these must now be examined.

According to the first version, feeling lonely after the marriage of her daughter, Béatrice de Montjean took up residence at Champtocé with the newlyweds. This did not suit Jean de Craon at all, nor Gilles. It was therefore decided that the most convenient way of getting rid of her was by finding her another husband. The most obvious choice was Jacques Meschin. Jean de Craon accordingly made suitable arrangements.

In view of subsequent events I find this explanation unlikely. Moreover it is doubtful whether Jean de Craon would have considered it in his grandson's interests for Béatrice de Montjean to remarry. There was always the possibility of an heir and that would complicate the problem of inheritance which, as always, he had so carefully thought out. It is also unlikely that he would have suggested Jacques Meschin as a likely candidate. He was a gentleman, he moved in court circles, he had made a pilgrimage to the Holy Land and had been knighted, but in an age with an acute sense of rank and hierarchy he could not be considered as belonging to the same class as his bride. It was not exactly a *mésalliance* but it was near to it. A more probable explanation is that the marriage came as an unpleasant surprise. The ceremony was a discreet one, not accompanied by the pomp and circumstance one would expect from anything arranged by Jean de Craon.

Whatever doubts surround the marriage itself there is none concerning the events which followed. The marriage settlement he had been forced to make to buy off Catherine's relatives still rankled in Jean de Craon's mind. He was determined to add the castles of Tiffauges and Pouzauges to the family estates. But Jacques Meschin was a vigorous man—another reason why Jean de Craon would not have wanted him in the family. He waited until Meschin was absent on business and made a deal with Jean de la Noë, captain of the guard at Tiffauges, to carry off Béatrice and her younger sister, for a suitable reward of course.

One evening de la Noë presented himself to the Countess and told her bluntly that she had been in Poitou too long and that it was time she went to Brittany to see her daughter. When the lady objected that it was nearly nightfall and hardly the time to set out on a lengthy journey his reply was very much to the point: 'Start moving or I'll truss you up like an old bundle and sling you across my horse.' This mediaeval courtesy put an effective stop to any further discussion. That night the two women rode under escort to Louroux-Bottereau where they were put under lock and key. The next day they were taken to Champtocé. On her arrival Béatrice was told that she must give up the castles that had been allotted to her under the marriage settlement. When she refused, Jean de Craon showed that he could be as brutal as his henchmen. She was informed that if she persisted in being obstinate she would be sewn up in a sack and thrown into the river. Whether they ever got as far as actually putting her in and dangling her over the water to prove their point is not certain. Béatrice, nothing daunted, refused to sign the documents that were required of her.

Jacques Meschin was anxious, naturally enough, to have his wife returned. He did not, however, carry valour so far as to present himself in person at the gates of Champtocé and demand her release. He sent three emissaries, including his brother Gilles. One of them caught a glimpse of the unfortunate lady through a window. A glimpse was all they had. They were told that they could not have the lady either 'by royal decree or Papal bull' unless she signed the required papers. They were then thrown into the deepest and foulest dungeon and left to rot without food or drink. *Noblesse oblige.*

At this point Anne de Sillé intervened, suggesting to her new husband that Béatrice should be returned to Tiffauges. This Jean de Craon did, but still kept the three emissaries firmly locked up. In the meantime he arranged the marriage of Gérard de la Noë to Béatrice's younger sister. He never 'welshed' on that kind of debt.

In the end Jacques Meschin was forced to give in. He paid a ransom for his three messengers, as was the custom, but his brother never recovered from his experiences and died shortly afterwards. A mediaeval dungeon was not the healthiest of places. The other two were also ill for a considerable time. He agreed to hand over both castles.

In the meantime the *Parlement* at Poitiers had been considering the matter and ruled that Meschin and his wife should choose one of the castles and the other should go to Gilles. They chose Pouzauges. Not that it made any difference. Gilles was already in possession of both and declared that he would not part with Pouzauges, on the feeble grounds that 'his wife bore the name of it in the world' and it was therefore a matter of honour.

But the authorities were not prepared to let the matter drop. Royal authority still meant something, or so they imagined. Adam de Cambray presented himself at Pouzauges to see that the judgement of king and *parlement* was carried out. Much had happened since a royal messenger had confronted Jean de Craon in 1413 to settle the dispute with the Loire watermen. Agincourt had happened. The disintegration of royal authority had happened. This time Jean de Craon did not withdraw gracefully. Adam de Cambray was brutally beaten up and sent back to Poitiers. Gilles and his grandfather were fined for *lèse-majesté* but even in 1453, thirteen years after Gilles' death, the fine was still not paid.

Gilles would never have been able to make the distinction between the state of royal authority in 1413 and 1423. His instinct would have been to use violence on each occasion. Jean de Craon was unable to hand on his own sense of judgment. What he had taught Gilles was that the Rais family was not subject to the laws of God or man. Gilles revelled in the use and abuse of his power; he was omnipotent. He was the heir to three vast fortunes, he was noble; he was Caesar, Nero and Caligula, outstripping his own monarch in wealth and power. The world was his and he was determined to enjoy it.

He had become the complete egotist, charming when he felt like it, overbearing, bullying and brutal when he was crossed. Now it was his grandfather's turn to feel the backlash. In 1420 Gilles was twenty and legally of age to take charge of his fortune. This he decided to do. We do not know how many quarrels this decision provoked but Jean de Craon certainly cannot have been happy. He had worked hard to amass a huge fortune and he must have been aware of his grandson's capacity for spending. But Gilles was adamant. The highly partisan account given by his relatives after his execution describes the matter thus:

> Item, that the said Gilles, when he had reached twenty or thereabouts, at the instigation of his servants and others who wished to enrich themselves upon his goods, took upon himself the administration of all his lands and estates and used them as he wished, taking no advice from his grandfather and no account of anything he said.

This is an exaggeration. Jean de Craon still had to initiate his grandson into court life and national politics, but for the next eight years the two gradually drifted apart.

Gilles' demand to control his property should not be confused with a mature desire for genuine responsibility. It was more like a child demanding unlimited access to his toys, refusing all parental injunctions as to moderation. And his wealth was enormous. Since his marriage his lands stretched inland from the Atlantic coast, south of Brittany, in an arc to the Channel coast north of St Aubin, inland along the Loire as far as Chinon and south as far as the River Sèvre. He had lands in Brittany, Anjou, Poitou and Maine. It was not a patrimony, it was a kingdom.

3

War and Court Politics

IN 1425 PREPARATIONS were made on the French side for a renewal of the Hundred Years War. If Charles VII had suffered from a busy, intriguing mother he found himself saddled with an equally active, if less malicious, mother-in-law, who was anxious for him to prove himself.

Charles is an enigmatic figure; portrayed by Shakespeare as an arrogant upstart and by Shaw as a timid ninny who finally makes the grade, he was probably neither. If he seemed ineffectual, circumstances were hardly in his favour. His mother had declared him a bastard, his father had disinherited him, a large part of his kingdom north of the Loire was in English hands, the Duke of Brittany could not make up his mind whether to recognise him or not, and the Duke of Burgundy was actively against him. His armies had been broken and there seemed little prospect of rebuilding them. Even his legal status was in doubt. Under the treaty signed at Troyes in 1420 Henry V had been recognised as the legal heir to Charles VI, and England and France were to be known as the double kingdom. The University of Paris, which was packed with pro-English scholars, had declared the treaty valid, and he himself was contemptuously known as 'le roi de Bourges' after the town in which he had for the time being established his capital. It was hardly a propitious start to a reign and Charles did not possess the kind of personality that inspired loyalty and devotion. None the less he had reserves of intelligence and ruthlessness as he was to show later. Behind his unprepossessing exterior was a considerable political sense which the more obviously endowed ignored at their peril. For the moment he was slighted and insulted, pushed from pillar to post. At times he was angry but there was no effective way he could demonstrate his displeasure. He learned patience and resignation early. But he survived, and his slow path to power and authority is littered with casualties, friend and foe alike, none of whom he lifted a finger to help.

His formidable mother-in-law had quite a different temperament and approach. Yolande d'Aragon was the daughter of Jean I of Aragon, and she had married Louis II, king of Naples, Sicily and Jerusalem, Duke of Anjou, Count of Provence. Her husband had died leaving her a young widow and she had shown considerable skill in defending her family's interests in the anarchic times during which she lived. In 1413, she married her daughter to Charles the Dauphin, thus placing herself in a central position to control the destinies of France. She was a woman of decision, energy and ambition, and she would have dearly liked to see some glimmer of these same qualities in her son-in-law. By 1424 she was impatient. It seemed unlikely that her daughter would ever mount the throne of France as her rightful queen. Charles had done nothing, except to move the court from Bourges to Poitiers, and so she decided that if her son-in-law would not make himself king, she would do it for him. The problem was to repossess the territories held by the English north of the Loire, including Paris. In her mind the key to any change in their fortunes was the province of Brittany, the key man, Jean V.

The wind, the Bible tells us, bloweth where it listeth. So did Jean V. He had switched from the French to the English side in the war ever since he had acceded to the Dukedom in 1404. Although nominally he owed allegiance to the throne of France he was much more closely connected with the English court since his mother had married Henry IV. But English fortunes were at a low ebb at the turn of the century; Henry was troubled by rebellious nobles, and so Jean V paid due homage to Charles VI. Three years later he changed his mind and signed a separate armistice with the English. In 1415, although he had promised support troops at Agincourt, they never arrived. They were 'prevented'. In 1420 he recognised the Treaty of Troyes, by which Charles the Dauphin was disinherited. In 1421 he switched again and, by the treaty of Sablé, returned to the French camp. In 1422, after the death of Henry V, he recognised the treaty of Troyes once more. In 1423, on April 17, he signed a treaty with England and Burgundy at Amiens, against the French.

To Yolande d'Aragon it seemed high time to end this game of diplomatic tennis, and to secure Jean V's loyalty once and for all. Her plan was a permanent treaty of alliance to be cemented in the usual manner, by a marriage between her son Louis III of Anjou and Isabelle de Bretagne, the Duke's daughter. It would not be an easy matter to negotiate; Jean V still had memories of the time he had spent in a dungeon as a result of the plot between Charles VII and the Penthièvre family. Who would be more likely to succeed than Jean de Craon? His skill could not have gone unnoticed in court circles, whatever the opinion of his moral character. Besides he was ideally placed. He had lands in Anjou, which made him technically a vassal to Yolande d'Aragon, and his grandson had vast estates in Brittany. Moreover Jean de Craon enjoyed very cordial relations with the Duke. She therefore approached him. The task must have appealed to him: he could exercise his talents for horse-trading once more and he could open his grandson's way to a prominent position at court. Besides he knew where his own interests lay. He had lost two castles to the English, Ambrières and Saint Aubain-Fosse-Louvain, which the English regent, Bedford, had assigned to one of his nobles on 14 June 1423. He therefore accepted.

Negotiations were protracted, as always, but the marriage contract was finally signed on 7 October 1425 at Saumur, in the presence of Jean V de Bretagne, Charles VII, Yolande d'Aragon, the betrothed couple, Jean de Craon and Gilles de Rais. It was Gilles' first contact with his sovereign and it marks his entry into the sphere of national affairs.

To reinforce the alliance, Arthur de Richemont, the Duke of Brittany's brother, was made Constable of France and given command of the army. He too, of course, was a stepson of Henry IV of England and his ties with Britain had been strengthened by his marriage to Marguerite de Bourgogne, which made him brother-in-law both to Philippe le Bon, Duke of Burgundy, and to the Duke of Bedford, the English Regent. Why then was he so resolutely pro-French? The reason was pique. He had gone to Bedford, asked for a command and had been turned down flat. He had immediately transferred his sympathies to Charles VII.

He was, of course, doubly indebted to Jean de Craon: first for arranging his ransom from the English at some speed, secondly for pulling off the negotiations which had led to his appointment. And, of course, any favours he owed Jean de Craon automatically went to his grandson, however much the two were beginning to quarrel about money and the management of the estates.

The facts about the backstairs bargaining and haggling that went on must remain a secret to us. They are rarely recorded; they blur the image of a noble aristocracy, guardian of its country's security and culture. What is certain is that from the moment that he received his appointment, de Richemont determined to find a place at court for his cousin, Georges de la Trémoille, who also happened to be Gilles' cousin on his grandfather's side.

Georges de la Trémoille, Comte de Guines, de Boulogne et d'Auvergne, Baron de Sully, de Craon, de Saint-Hermine and later de l'Isle-Bouchard, rotund, sleek in mind and body, had waited for some time to make his mark at court. He was rich and powerful and yet he had never enjoyed the position to which he felt entitled. This was probably due, in large part, to the fact that he had spent much of his life at the court of the Duke of Burgundy, who regularly sided with the English in the Hundred Years War, and thanks to whose help, the English were now in possession of Paris. However, La Trémoille had fought for France at Agincourt, had been captured and quickly ransomed. He returned to the home of the Duc de Berry, the wealthy patron of the arts, where he had been living since his departure from Burgundy. He seems to have found particular favour with the Duchess for, on the death of her husband, after a suitable period of mourning, she married him on 16 November 1416. She died childless in 1422, leaving him the income from all her vast estates. He now had everything he needed to make a name for himself at court, except someone to sponsor him. And who better than his newly appointed cousin?

Whether Jean de Craon encouraged de Richemont to advance La Trémoille we cannot be certain, but there appears to have been an exchange of favours between de Craon and La Trémoille which suggests a marriage of interests.

However desirable de Richemont's appointment as Constable might have been from a political point of view, Charles did not take to the man, and neither did anybody else. He was crude, boorish, and, it seemed at times, deliberately vulgar. The French court was nothing if not sophisticated and this man, with his coarse manners and his quite unfashionably simple and violently held religious faith, seemed little better than a savage.

Still, it was not for his manners that de Richemont had been appointed but for his abilities as a soldier. He lost no time in raising troops and decided to launch his first attack against the English at Saint-James-de-Beuvron. It is not certain whether Gilles was present at this battle. The Abbé Bossard places him there without any question. Emile Gabory, on the other hand, disagrees quite categorically, citing the lack of documentary evidence, and even goes so far as to describe Gilles' presence at Saint-James as pure 'invention'. It seems to me that M. Gabory is being over-emphatic on slender grounds. Documentary evidence in this period is neither complete nor entirely reliable. Moreover, after his disgrace, Gilles' name tended to be excluded from official or literary accounts—people could be 'unpersoned' long before the twentieth century. Looking back at Gilles' career, knowing how famous, and infamous, he was to become, we are surprised not to find his name mentioned at every turn, but in 1426 he was just another lion cub, even if he did have a great deal of money, and not everyone who participated in a battle, particularly in a minor capacity, would find a mention in the Chronicles. Gilles' name is, in fact, conspicuous by its absence, suggesting a quiet glossing over of his rôle. It is only due to the evidence that Dunois, the Bastard of Orléans, gave at the Rehabilitation Trial of Joan of Arc that we learn of his presence at the siege of Orléans.

It is difficult to imagine Gilles, with his need of violence, sitting at home while the first campaign against the English was launched, particularly considering how near his grandfather was to the centre of things. And it would certainly have been to his advantage to have been side by side with the new Constable in his first sortie.

Whether he was there or not, Gilles would have learned two

valuable lessons from this battle: first, always to have enough money to pay your troops; second, always be well informed. It was on these two points that the attack foundered.

It started promisingly enough. De Richemont's forces out-numbered the English garrison by twenty to one. Unfortunately, he had to fight not only the occupying forces but also treachery at home. Jean de Malestroit, Chancellor of the Duchy of Brittany, had always been opposed to the alliance with France. He was violently anglophile and wanted to stabilise relations with the young Henry VI. Equally opposed to de Richemont was Pierre de Giac, the king's favourite, who had not taken kindly to the new Constable's arrival or to his sudden rise to eminence, threatening as it did his own position. Both these enemies in their own way set about sabotaging de Richemont's efforts. Jean de Malestroit withheld the necessary funds with which de Richemont hoped to pay his troops, while de Giac re-routed essential food supplies. Unpaid and unfed, the French army was demoralised before the battle even began. Moreover tactically their position was less than ideal. They were divided down the middle by a large pond and a highway, so that two separate camps had to be established. Communication between them was not easy, nor was co-ordination of effort. De Richemont could not see what half his army was doing. Men were deserting, and de Richemont, realising how precarious his position was, decided to attack before the situation deteriorated further.

The attack began with a preliminary bombardment which lasted a week. Then, on March 6, the assault proper took place at the two points on opposite sides of the town, where serious breaches had been made in the English defences. The defending garrison fought bravely in the expectation of being relieved within a very short space of time by reinforcements which were due to arrive. The battle had been raging for some three or four hours when the English saw a body of soldiers advancing in the distance. Taking them to be the support they were ex-pecting, they left the town by another gate and attacked the Breton troops in the rear, crying 'Suffolk and Salisbury!' The Breton troops were taken completely by surprise and their panic was increased when they too saw the troops riding up from the distance. They abandoned the attack and ran as fast as they could to their own camp. The English pursued, raining arrows down upon them, driving many of them into the pond where they drowned. The Breton troops lost sixty men killed, fifty prisoner and a large number of their banners.

Meanwhile de Richemont, leading his troops on the other side of the town, cut off from half his army, was unaware of what had happened. The troops who had been approaching from the distance were in fact men of his own whom he had sent to Avranges to reconnoitre. They were completely unaware of the panic they had caused. When de Richemont saw the men from the other half of the army rushing to find refuge in his camp, he realised that it was useless to continue the struggle. He might have been able to retreat in good order and regroup his forces, if luck had been with him. The English had suffered considerable losses on their side and were in no position to follow up their advantage. Unfortunately there was another panic in de Richemont's camp during the night, which dashed any hopes he might have had.

What caused this sudden fright we do not know, but it was now every man for himself. Men were running wildly in all directions, trying to save their own skins. Tents were set on fire, and de Richemont himself was obliged to retreat if he did not want to be burned alive. He mounted his horse and tried to rally the panicking mass of soldiers, but he was thrown and almost trampled underfoot. He remounted and tried to rally sufficient men to save the cannon but it was no use. Finally he was obliged to follow his retreating men. The battle ended in total ignominy.

De Richemont had no doubt in his own mind as to the cause of his disgrace; he was aware of the machinations of Jean de Malestroit and Pierre de Giac and he was hot for revenge. Before returning to court he passed through Nantes, seized Jean de Malestroit, took him to Chinon and threw him into prison. But he could prove nothing, and under pressure from de Malestroit's many friends at court he was forced to release him. As for de Giac he would have to be removed, permanently. But such a move required time, planning, and a favourable opportunity.

If de Richmont was unpopular so was de Giac. He was overbearing, insolent; he plundered the royal coffers to pay off those friends who protected him against his many enemies. He gave de Richemont further cause to hate him by blocking every move he made to create an alliance between his brother-in-law Philippe le Bon, Duke of Burgundy, and the king. Such an alliance would have deprived the English of one of their main supports. But de Giac wanted none of it; he could only see it as a move which would undermine his influence with the king. And without that he was as good as dead. In fact, he was as good as dead anyway.

Not that de Giac deserved any sympathy. Apart from being generally unpleasant and raiding the royal coffers, which after all was not an uncommon practice, he had murdered his first wife in a particularly brutal manner. Having made one of her ladies in waiting, Catherine de l'Isle-Bouchard, pregnant, he poisoned his wife, threw her on to a horse and rode through the woods with her until she was dead; then he threw her body to the ground, leaving it to be devoured by wolves. Shortly afterwards he married Catherine. He could hardly complain then if he received the summary justice which Arthur de Richemont was more than willing to supply.

De Richemont canvassed opinion. First of all he obtained the support of his cousin Georges de la Trémoille, who had already become Catherine de l'Isle-Bouchard's lover. Catherine herself, apparently, was not unwilling to see her husband go. He may also have discussed the matter with his brother-in-law Philippe le Bon when they were together at Moulins negotiating the new alliance. All those courtiers not in de Giac's immediate circle were certainly in favour, and so was Yolande d'Aragon, who was not willing to see important matters of state held up for the conceit and arrogance of a selfish favourite. It was generally agreed then to remove Pierre de Giac once and for all. Plans were laid in great secrecy, and when de Richemont finally joined the court which had removed to Issoudun neither the king nor his detested friend had any idea that there was a plot afoot.

Saturday, February 8 was the day fixed for their move. On the evening of the 7th de Richemont had all the keys of the town handed over to him on the pretext that he intended going very early to Notre-Dame-de-Bourg-de-Déols. He told his men to come for him as soon as everything was ready. Before first light on the 8th he was sitting in the chapel when his men arrived. Mass was just about to begin but de Richemont left the priest to intone his prayers to the cold morning air. He then joined the apparently ever faithful Georges de la Trémoille and d'Albret who were waiting for him with a company of archers.

Everything was quiet. De Richemont and his men crept along the corridors until they came to de Giac's room. They broke down the door with hammer blows. De Giac was in bed with his new wife. In the dark he could not see who it was who had burst into his room but when he was informed that it was de Richemont he knew his chances of survival were very small. He was hauled naked out of bed, given just sufficient time to pull on boots and a dressing gown. Catherine de l'Isle Bouchard leapt naked from her bed and began to attack the soldiers but only to protect the valuables in the room from their plundering hands. Whatever agreement she had made with La Trémoille, it certainly did not entail financial loss.

De Giac was hauled off, half clad, bundled into a small carriage and taken to the town gates. In the meantime the king and his guards had been aroused by the noise and soon learned what was happening. Charles despatched his men to the gates in an attempt to save his friend, but de Richemont sent them straight back with the comment that he was acting for the king's own good. Charles must have reflected wryly on the number of people who claimed to do precisely that and made his life miserable in the process. At this point Alain Giron, Robert de Montauban and several others of de Richemont's accomplices arrived with a hundred lancers, making quite sure that no one would be able to interfere with the execution of the plan. De Richemont and La Trémoille went to Bourges, but de Giac was sent under escort to Dun-le-Roi with a message to the Bailiff of the town that he was to be tried for the murder of his wife and malversation of royal funds.

De Giac made a full confession, as the chronicler Gruel relates:

> He confessed so many crimes that there was great marvelling, among others the murder of his wife, who was great with child, the fruit being in her womb. More than this he confessed that he had given one of his hands to the devil,

so as to summon him and be served by him. When he was condemned he asked that the said hand should be cut off before he was put to death.

Having confessed so obligingly, de Giac then tried to buy his way out:

[He] offered to give my lord Constable 100,000 *écus*, his wife, his children and all those places in which he kept hostages as surety that he would never again approach within twenty leagues of the king.

The offer was transmitted to de Richemont in Bourges, but the Constable, as Gilles was to learn later, had a fanatical hatred of anything that smacked of witchcraft and he sent a message back to de Giac saying that he would not let him go for anything in the world and that he deserved to die. The message was accompanied by an executioner. De Giac's right hand was cut off, as he had requested, in an attempt to save his soul from hell, although he must have entertained a very liberal idea of divine mercy if he did not imagine that was his destination already. He was then sewn up in a sack and drowned in the River Auron. His body was later fished out of the water and buried by his men.

Charles, to say the least, was not pleased and de Richemont spent a great deal of time trying to placate him, giving him a full review of de Giac's crimes. Charles, of course, did nothing and in a short while de Richemont confidently announced that the king 'felt quite happy about it'. He was wrong, the king did not; but he needed de Richemont, and so he let the matter drop. He knew he was hopelessly outnumbered, and the lesson must have been driven home when La Trémoille married de Giac's second wife, Catherine de l'Isle-Bouchard, a short time later. He was not however prepared to live entirely friendless, with no one to confide in during the long evenings, and it was not difficult to obtain the king's favour. All anyone needed to do was to show him a little warmth and consideration.

If de Richemont hoped to replace de Giac with his cousin La Trémoille he was slow off the mark, because the king's favour lighted on Camus de Beaulieu, a young man who commanded a company of the royal guard and who moreover owed his position to de Richemont himself. He had no political ambitions like his predecessor but he was at pains to exclude anyone who might diminish his influence with the king, and that included his patron. Beaulieu proved to be no more popular than de Giac had been—can a royal favourite ever be liked? Yolande d'Aragon did not approve of him, neither did the other nobles of the court. It was not long before complaints reached the ears of the Constable, who was not exactly well disposed towards his recalcitrant protégé. He, too, would have to be removed but there were other, more pressing affairs of state to settle first. De Richemont had not been appointed to butcher in turn all the king's favourites but to mount a successful campaign against the English. So far he had not done very well.

In the early part of 1427 Yolande d'Aragon appointed Jean de Craon Lieutenant-General of Anjou. Whether this was entirely gratitude for his success in handling neogitations or whether she was put up to it by de Richemont and La Trémoille is not certain, but it seems probable that La Trémoille had some hand in it, for he was making his presence felt in court circles, although he enjoyed no official position. Jean de Craon's appointment entailed the levying and command of troops. This was obviously beyond him at seventy, so the task fell to Gilles who set about raising five companies to participate in the various harassing raids that were being mounted against the English, and in which de Richemont was actively concerned.

The Constable had not forgotten, however, the necessity of removing the king's current favourite and replacing him with someone reliable, like his cousin La Trémoille. And he was not prepared this time to go through the pretence of a trial for someone as insignificant as Beaulieu. A straightforward assassination would do.

On this occasion the king, quite by accident, was given a ringside seat. The court had moved again. By June 1427 it was back once more in Poitiers, where the castle gave a fine view of the river and the surrounding country. Arthur de Richemont had given one of his men, Jean de Brossé, the task of removing the new favourite. De Brossé found the simplest method was to enlist the aid of Beaulieu's so-called best friend, Jean de la Granche, who agreed to set up the victim, doubtless in the expectation of future favours from the Constable.

One day Beaulieu and his friend de la Granche were taking a walk in the fields by the river Clain when half a dozen men previously posted there by de Brosse leapt out at them. Charles, who happened to be looking out of his window at the time, saw the incident. One man, de la Granche, escaped unhurt, but the second man—Charles was too far away to identify him as his favourite—was cut down, blood streaming from great gashes in his head. His hand was then hacked off for no special reason, unless it was to leave no one in any doubt as to who was behind the murder. Once they were quite sure Beaulieu was dead the attackers took to their heels. It was only later that Charles realised that Beaulieu had been the victim, when he saw de la Granche leading his friend's mule back to the castle. He immediately called out the guard and ordered them to pursue the criminals and bring them to justice, but, needless to say, they were never found.

This time de Richemont took no chances on the king's favour lighting on another unsuitable figure. He proposed that Charles take La Trémoille as his friend and confidant. He painted a glowing picture of his cousin's wealth and devotion to the crown. Charles received the suggestion with a faint smile and the remark, 'A pretty story, cousin. But you'll live to regret it. I know him better than you do.' He did, and within a matter of months events were to prove him right.

While this murderous struggle for power was in progress at court Gilles was distinguishing himself in the field. For once, there is no disagreement about the part he played in the military campaigns of spring and summer 1427. He had levied his five companies and he was ready for glory. Not that Jean de Craon was willing to allow his comparatively inexperienced grandson to expose himself needlessly to danger. He gave him a mentor and guide in the person of Guillaume de la Jumellière, an experienced soldier, who would prevent Gilles from making wrong decisions. He was suitably rewarded for his services and his name appears in Gilles' accounts under the name of Monseigneur de Martigné. The five new companies joined up with the force of Ambroise de Loré, a veteran of great skill and doubtful honesty, who seems to have been in general charge of operations. Among Gilles' other companions was a young nobleman called Beaumanoir, with whom Gilles was to form a close friendship.

Gilles had never been one to stint himself. Doubtless he had already made an impression on those public and state occasions when he had appeared with his grandfather. Certainly the Abbé Bossard thinks so, and it is unlikely that, if he lived with such opulence at home, he would do less in public. For his first appearance as a military commander he made a special effort. He was always surrounded by a huge retinue all magnificently clad; his troops were well paid and provided for, thus ensuring their undying loyalty; and he employed more than the usual number of spies who were exceptionally well paid and kept him constantly supplied with information. He had learned the lessons of de Richemont's failure and had no intention of being caught in the same way.

Gilles did not take long to prove himself, and his arrival, with five companies of fresh troops, gave new impetus to the campaign.

It was success all the way. Saint-Jean de Mortier, Ramefort and the castle of Malicorne were taken by the combined efforts of Gilles, Beaumanoir and de Loré. Gilles then rode to Montargis with Beaumanoir, joined forces with de Richemont and La Hire and took the town. He then rode back, still with his new-found companion Beaumanoir, to join de Loré who was preparing an assault on the English stronghold at Lude. The garrison there was commanded by the famous English captain, Blackburn, who had sworn to defend the castle to the death.

It was not an easy objective. The garrison was large, the towers solidly built and the ramparts practically unscalable. Gilles and his companions set up their cannon on the surrounding heights and unleashed a heavy and prolonged bombardment. The signal was then given for the attack.

This was not a period in which generals followed the course of a battle from the safety of a reinforced bunker, moving plastic buttons on a squared map, as though the whole incident had no more importance than a game of chess. Commanders led their men, and it was at Lude that Gilles displayed those qualities of dash and reckless bravery that were to make him famous. Perhaps he thought he was invulnerable; perhaps he was endowed with a magical belief in his own power to win. It would hardly have been surprising. At all events, as soon as the signal was given, Gilles rushed to the castle walls; he was one of the first to arrive at the top and there he found himself face to face with Captain Blackburn, no mean adversary. The confrontation was swift, and in a matter of minutes Blackburn lay dead at Gilles' feet. At this, English morale collapsed totally and the castle was quickly taken.

Gilles was the hero, and he was treated like one. When the question of disposing of prisoners was discussed his word seems to have been final. He spared many of the English, but the Frenchman who was found to have collaborated with them was summarily executed. To his companions this must have seemed like a waste of good ransom money but Gilles was adamant.

An attempt was then made to relieve Le Mans. They were let into the town by loyal citizens but the English garrison under Talbot proved too strong for them and they were forced to withdraw. None the less they returned to court in triumph.

At court much had changed. While Gilles had been covering himself with glory his cousin La Trémoille had been active in his own interest. True to Charles' prediction he had set about destroying his cousin and patron de Richemont. This was not difficult. De Richemont was unpopular with the king, and after his defeat at Saint-James-de-Beuvron his brother Jean V had once more gone over to the English. His position was completely undermined. La Trémoille had himself made Chamberlain, a position equivalent to that of Prime Minister. Following the classic pattern of every favourite before him, he warded off anyone who might endanger his influence with the king, and proceeded to put his arms elbow-deep into the royal coffers, though with rather more subtlety than some others. He was at the top at last. Then, seeing his rich, young, naïve cousin arrive at court in a blaze of glory, he decided to take an interest in his career.

4

Joan of Arc

THERE WAS NOTHING altruistic about Georges de la Trémoille's
motives. He realised how vulnerable he was. Like every favourite before him, he needed powerful allies. The court was divided
between those who supported him and those who supported de
Richemont. The main source of opposition, he was aware, could
come from Yolande d'Aragon, the king's all-powerful mother-
in-law, and it would only be a matter of time before they came
into open conflict in their efforts to control royal policy. De
Richemont was not a man to give up easily, either. He had got
rid of two favourites already; he would not hesitate to remove
a third. A counter-attack might come at any moment.

   La Trémoille need to mobilise his forces. There were those
he could bribe with favours, but their support would be dependent on his control of privilege and they might desert him without warning if it seemed he might lose the fight. He needed
someone powerful and someone who would be known as *his*
man. The obvious choice was his cousin Gilles, the only man
in an impoverished court rich enough to maintain a private
army. He was also very popular at court; he was handsome, gay
and witty, he dressed better than anyone else, and he was entirely
without scruple. Everyone was aware that he was a dangerous man to cross, despite his courtly graces. If La Trémoille
could count on his cousin's open support then his own position
would be much more secure. Besides he was convinced he knew
just how to manipulate him. He knew that Gilles' sole concern
was his own immediate pleasure. If he could keep him amused
and cover him with glittering honours he could lead him politically in any direction he chose. Manipulating him would be no
more difficult than giving sweets to a delinquent child. When,
many years later, La Trémoille was accused of having exploited

the worst side of Gilles' nature he replied, 'It is good to encourage him to be evil.'

Gilles himself was quite happy to link his interests with his cousin. It is doubtful whether he was really aware of what this implied but it enabled him to show off. He appears to have been in happy mood. He was a hero and he had just taken a ten-year-old boy, Etienne Corillaut, known familiarly as Poitou, into his service as a page. Poitou was handsome, one of the many 'little angels' Gilles so delighted in. He was to serve his master well over the next thirteen years, and go to the stake with him.

For a year nothing happened until in the early summer of 1428 de Richemont made his expected attempt to oust La Trémoille from power. The trial of strength took place at Bourges, Charles' capital. De Richemont was convinced that the townsfolk were sympathetic to him and invited them to hand over the administration to him and his men. News of this move reached La Trémoille and both he and the king immediately despatched letters forbidding them to admit de Richemont within their walls. None the less the Constable's men marched in and, apart from one small pocket of resistance, were generally welcomed. They at once seized the treasury and began to levy taxes. To all intents and purposes an alternative government had been set up.

La Trémoille quickly raised an army and marched on Bourges with the king. Although there is no direct documentary evidence there is every reason to assume that Gilles was part of this army. In the event no fighting took place. On July 17 both sides agreed to a negotiated settlement in which La Trémoille made a series of concessions he had no intention of honouring. But for the moment his position was secure.

It is typical of the period that while the French were involved in their private squabbles, national disaster was threatening. The English had passed over to the offensive in a determined effort to end the war once and for all. They intended to break the stalemate which left them in control north of the Loire, while Charles was in possession of the land south of the river. They planned to take Orléans then push down into Le Berry and drive Charles out of his last refuge. If they succeeded, apart from the purely military gain, the effect on French morale, already low, would be disastrous. Salisbury had landed at Calais on June 24 with fresh troops but the French did not turn aside from their own internal struggle. Even after the July agreement de Richemont continued to harry Charles' troops in Poitou so that the English were able to march unopposed to Orléans. By October the siege had begun.

An attempt was made to relieve the town in February 1429 but it was a typically disastrous enterprise. The French forces were as usual unco-ordinated and disorganised, with each individual commander trying to grab the victory for himself. The result was total defeat. The French army attacked the supply train bringing herrings for the English to eat during Lent. The battle took place among the broken barrels and was known afterwards, mockingly, as the Day of the Herrings. The stench of fish was added to the sour smell of defeat. After that, most of the French commanders abandoned the town, leaving only Dunois the Bastard behind to afford the inhabitants any kind of protection. The English forces settled in, built wooden fortresses as protection against French sorties and the weather, and waited patiently for the town to fall. Charles and his court were at Chinon, amusing themselves. They were aware of the gravity of the situation yet no one seemed able to do anything. If Orléans, and France, was to be saved a miracle was needed.

A miracle had been announced. Advance news had arrived of Joan the Maid who was coming from Vaucouleurs under the protection of Robert de Baudricourt. She claimed that she would raise the siege of Orléans, crown the Dauphin in Reims cathedral and even, according to some, rescue Charles d'Orléans, who was a prisoner of war in England. How she was to do this last was not stated. The court was alive with rumour and gossip. Old prophecies were dug up and reinterpreted— sayings of Merlin, passages from the Venerable Bede and, in particular, the predictions of Marie d'Avignon, a woman who had suddenly appeared at the court of Charles VI towards the end of the previous century.

In her prophetic utterings she had stated that many calamities would befall France and she claimed to have seen a vision of many weapons. At first she had been afraid that she might be called upon to bear these arms herself but it was not her task to deliver the kingdom of France. A maid would come. Yet another prophecy stated that just as France had been lost by a woman—Isabeau de Bavière—so she would be saved by another. That woman seemed to be Joan.

In view of subsequent events we must assume that Gilles was at Chinon during this time. He, more than anyone else, would have been excited by the slow build-up to the Maid's arrival. All his life he had a passion for the dramatic and the theatrical, and here was drama on a cosmic scale, the eruption of the supernatural into human affairs.

Joan's first encounter with the Dauphin had all the appearance of careful stage management. The room was lit with fifty torches and the whole court was assembled. Joan made her entrance and, according to Jean Chartier, Charles VII's official historian, curtseyed as though she had been doing it all her life. She was a striking woman who dressed, and in many ways behaved, like a man and yet had feminine qualities of compassion and tenderness. Everyone who met her was impressed by the force of her personality. She had 'charisma'. Moreover she provided a minor wonder by recognising the king who was hiding among his courtiers, trying to look inconspicuous, and doubtless succeeding. When she addressed him he denied that he was the king, pointing to one of his courtiers with the words, 'You are mistaken, *there* is the king.' But Joan persisted, calling him 'Gentle Dauphin'.

More embroidered versions of this first encounter exist. In one it was said that the Comte de Clermont occupied the throne and pretended to be the king; in another it was Gilles himself who sat there. This second version was adopted by Bernard Shaw in *Saint Joan*. Certainly Gilles, who never wore anything except the finest materials, would have looked much more like the conventional idea of a king than anyone else present. But no real foundation for the legend exists.

Joan then spent two hours with the Dauphin, during which time she revealed to him a secret only known to herself. She stubbornly refused to say what it was right up to her death. Many years after she had been burned Charles stated that she had told him of a private prayer he had made concerning, significantly enough, his legitimacy. After Joan had spoken to him the king wept. She was taken to a room in the palace and examined by Yolande d'Aragon to see whether her claim to be a virgin was genuine. It was.

Despite the impression she had made, Charles decided that before he handed over the army to her she must be examined in matters of theology, to make sure she had come from God and not the devil. She was interrogated for three weeks in Poitiers by a group of clerics whom she treated, as far as one can judge from her remarks to the Duc d'Alençon, her future companion-in-arms, with an amused contempt. They pronounced themselves satisfied. They too, of course, had been preconditioned by the myths and legends that were current. Besides, everyone badly needed Joan's story to be true. Who else was going to save their skins? But who, in fact, was she?

Of all the people who influenced Gilles' life, Joan is the most controversial and the most enigmatic. The events of her life are not in doubt; they are more than adequately documented, in one sense at least. But the Joan accepted by the modern world is the result of a slow evolution of opinion and myth-making which has taken five hundred years to complete. And so important was the relationship between Gilles de Rais and Joan the Maid that some writers have constructed their whole interpretation of his life around it, often with highly misleading results. But the fact remains that for the rest of the year 1429 Joan's life and Gilles' life are the same and it was through his association with her that he achieved fame and glory. The question of Joan's beliefs and the nature of her mission must, therefore, be raised again and answers indicated even if they cannot be asserted.

Certainly the events which followed Joan's arrival at Chinon look like a set of carefully arranged tests to prove that she was not what, in fact, she most probably was, a witch. It was Dr Margaret Murray who early in the 'twenties first advanced the theory that Joan was a member of a witch cult. To be sure the English had always accused her of satanic practices, and Shakespeare shows her evoking demons, but Dr Murray's emphasis was rather different. Despite an unfortunate tendency to exaggerate and extend her theories in all directions she did adduce a considerable body of evidence. Her basic work has since been developed and given a much more closely reasoned form by Dr Ian Grimble, who has scrutinised the trial records, and abandoned the more 'vapid theorisings' of which Dr Murray has been accused.

In Dr Murray's theory witchcraft is the survival of an older religion, which persists into the Christian era. Its god is a horned fertility god, later identified by the Christian church with the devil. The Old Religion did in fact merge with orthodox Christian beliefs, so that confusion existed at many levels, rather in the way the South American Indians, while nominally remaining Catholic, incorporate many archaic beliefs and practices into their theology. The Old Religion was organised into covens of thirteen members, one of the most important members being known, significantly, as the Maid. Strong evidence suggests that when the devil appeared it was in fact a member of the coven dressed to represent him. The idea that a human could represent, and to all intents and purposes *be* a divine agent was central to this system of belief. If Joan was a member of the Old Religion, and the Maid of her coven, she would have accepted this idea quite readily, and also most probably confused the divine beings of her own theology with the Christian saints. The Saints Catherine, Margaret and Michael, who guided her and instructed her, were on this basis real people able to communicate directly with her. Joan's knowledge of military matters and her skill as a soldier can thus be explained by the instruction she received from whichever member of the cult represented the Archangel Michael.

A natural corollary to this hypothesis is the existence of the cult at the French court, where Michael, in his genuine identity, would have been an accepted figure. In her evidence at the trial Joan made reference to seeing the people of 'her party' among the 'Christians', a significant distinction. Moreover by proclaiming herself as the Maid, she would have rendered quite plainly to everyone where she stood in theological terms. The Duke of Bedford took the hint, referring to her exploitation of superstitious beliefs in a letter of protest to Charles during the siege of Orléans. During her trial Joan always spoke of God, or My Lord, never of Jesus, or Christ: she refused to say the Paternoster, which witches were supposed to be unable to do. She also asked for many questions to be giving to her in writing, stipulating a delay of a certain number of days after which she would reply. Joan herself was illiterate, so that her demand for written questions suggests that she wanted to be instructed in her answers. It is obvious also from the trial record that she had been told to keep her mouth shut.

This theory could be verified if it were possible to state positively who the Saints Catherine, Margaret and Michael were. Unfortunately this is not possible. However it does account for a number of curious anomalies and for the ambiguous attitude of the Catholic Church. Pope Pius II was not at all convinced of Joan's orthodoxy, wondering whether her story was the result of divine intervention or some more human agency. His guarded but significant conclusion was that her case was perhaps a matter for 'wonder rather than for faith'. It also explains La Trémoille's unfavourable attitude to her 'mission' and his continuous attempts to undermine all her efforts.

His prime concern was his own position and influence. If Joan's arrival was carefully staged by members of the cult and her story accepted on grounds of expediency by other members of the court, including his enemy Yolande d'Aragon, he stood to lose everything, for then it would be those who were manipulating her who would control policy, and not himself. Moreover, since she had passed all the tests that had been carefully devised, the next step was for her to take charge of the army, which would give her and her friends absolute control.

He decided to make use of his cousin Gilles once more. Only his wealth and influence could counterbalance the opposition forces. But this time their alliance was to be put on a formal basis; the gentlemen's agreement of the preceding two years was no longer sufficient. On 8 April 1429 Gilles signed the following document, proclaiming his allegiance to his cousin:

We Gilles, Lord of Rais and Pouzauges, certify, in gratitude for the great good, honours, courtesies done to us by our most honoured and puissant lord Monseigneur Georges, lord of La Trémoille, Sully and Craon, and in hope of things to come, and for the good and ancient love and confidence that in his courtesy he has shown us, and for many other considerations by which we feel ourselves bound in reason to him, by bonds of lineage as much as other, have promised, sworn and covenanted on the faith and oath of our body, and in fear of our honour, and forthwith promise him by this present that in all his matters and needs, and every time he shall require it of us... we shall serve him with all our strength, to the death or to the life, towards all and against all lords and others, none excepted... in the good grace and love of the king and in his service, and maintain him in the state in which he is at present, or greater...

We in sign of confirmation have signed this present with our own hand and sealed with our own seal, bearing our arms.

Given at Chinon the 8th day of April in the year One Thousand Four Hundred Nine and Twenty, after Easter.
Gilles de Rais.

The next step was to place Gilles in charge of the army that was to accompany the Maid to Orléans: 'About the end of April my Lord of Rais, Marshal of France [sic], and many other captains, as well as common soldiers were assigned to the Maid.'* Among the other captains was Gilles' old comrade-in-arms Ambroise de Loré. The bulk of his troops were drawn from Maine and Anjou and included his cousins Robert de Briqueville and Gilles and Michel de Sillé.

While Gilles was concerned with the practical problems of raising an army Joan continued her magical progress through the countryside. No effort was spared to surround her with a supernatural aura. From Chinon she went to Tours. There she had a special suit of white armour made. She also ordered two personal banners, one large and one small, which were supplied by Hamish Power, one of the many Scots living in the region. On the larger of the two banners appeared the figure of Christ flanked by two angels. (This design had apparently been given to her by her 'Voices'.) She then asked for the sword that would be found in the church of Sainte Catherine de Fierbois; it would be recognised by the five crosses engraved on the blade. The presence of this weapon had also been 'revealed' to her. The prophecies of Merlin had been revived before her arrival, so it was natural that her choice of sword should have Arthurian overtones. She did not, however, draw it from the stone. It

Chronique de l'Etablissement de la Procession du 8 mai.

was, in fact, so rusty that it needed a great deal of cleaning to make it serviceable. But it was the gesture not the object that was important; the symbol, not the reality. Indeed, in its own mind, the French court had already assigned her a purely symbolic rôle. Her function was to inspire, not to make decisions; in this, at least, La Trémoille and his enemies agreed, though for different motives.

Joan was hedged in on all sides, by those of 'her party' who were guiding her, and by those supporting La Trémoille who were trying to limit her influence. Gilles was to command her army; Jean d'Aulon, another of Georges de la Trémoille's appointments, was to be her squire. An Augustinian monk, Jean Pasquerel, accompanied her everywhere, and her two brothers, who appear to have been easily manipulated, were brought from Lorraine. The preliminaries were over. Now she was to be brandished before the populace in an attempt to put new heart into them.

From Tours she travelled to Blois with a convoy of supplies under the command of the Marshal de Boussac. At Blois she was joined by Gilles and the main force of the army, and also by La Hire and Xantrailles. However, before the army began the march on Orléans Joan gave a series of orders which were perfectly in line with her own thinking but totally against current practice. First she got rid of the regimental whores; they were given twenty-four hours to marry or quit. Secondly she forbade all swearing or blasphemy. This was particularly directed against La Hire whose foul language was notorious. During the campaign he only let fly in private. Thirdly all the soldiers were to go to confession. Finally there was to be no pillaging or terrorisation of the populace. All food obtained from the local peasants was to be paid for. It was evident that this campaign was going to be very different from the preceding ones, whatever anyone might say.

The army set out from Blois in formal procession. At the head were the clergy, singing the *Veni Creator,* then came the troops headed by Gilles and de Boussac, together with Louis de Culan, La Hire and Ambroise de Loré. The supply train brought up the rear.

In the town of Blois many carts, great and small, were laden with wheat and also a large number of cattle, sheep, cows, swine, and other victuals were taken, and Joan the Maid set out, as did the Captains for Orléans, passing through the Sologne [i.e. south of the Loire]. And they lay one night in the open and on the morrow came the Maid and the Captains with the supplies before the town of Orléans.

The food supplies had been gathered together by Yolande d'Aragon but in a last-minute panic it was realised that there was no money to pay for them. Charles sold off his last remaining jewels and borrowed a large sum from La Trémoille, probably money that had originally come from his own coffers. It is possible that Gilles himself may have made a contribution. At all events the money was found and word went quickly round the army that they were to be paid for the first time in years. This gave a considerable boost to morale and the French troops approached Orléans with a feeling of confidence.

Militarily the situation had been stagnating for several months. The town was built on the north bank of the river and

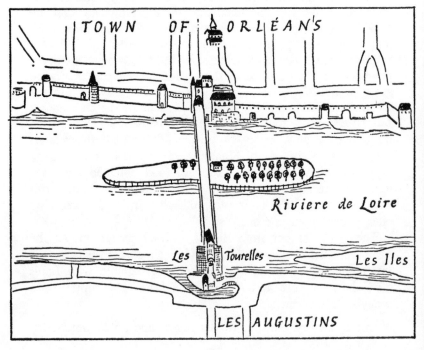

connected with the southern side by a bridge. The bridge itself passed over a small island mid-stream and its southern extremity was protected by the fort of Les Tourelles. The main part of the town was protected by a garrison of a thousand men, supported by the local militia, plus artillery equal in fire-power to the English. Dunois, the Bastard of Orléans, was in charge of the defences.

Early on in the campaign the English had attacked the fort of Les Tourelles and taken it after heavy fighting. Dunois had then ordered the destruction of the bridge. In consequence the town had been completely isolated from the south bank. After that, no serious fighting had taken place. The English, whose army was about 3,500 men, realised that they could not take the town by frontal attack and settled down for a long wait in the hope that they could starve it out.

In fact the town received constant reinforcements and supplies from the surrounding countryside and could hold out indefinitely. The English for their part spent most of their time in the wooden forts they had constructed and contented themselves with occasional sorties. Tactically their position was far from advisable, as Jean de Bueil pointed out in his novel *Le Jouvencel*. They were split into small groups which made concerted action almost impossible. A relieving army could pick them off one by one.

But no one seemed unduly worried. The stalemate was typical of the period. For all the inherent dangers of the situation for France as a growing nation, war was still a game to be played for the maximum of glory and the minimum of discomfort. Engagements were broken off every time they looked like becoming too costly or serious. The opposing generals exchanged courtesies. Suffolk on one occasion sent Dunois a dish of figs by a herald with a request that a length of black velvet to line his robe should be sent in return. Dunois obliged.

All this meant nothing to Joan. Her approach was much more forthright and radical. She did not intend to play the game by set rules. Her intention was to march straight to Orléans and attack immediately while her soldiers were full of enthusiasm and fresh from the confessional. She was bitterly angry when she discovered that she had been deliberately misled as to the route the army had taken. She had expected to march along the north bank and come directly to the town. Instead she found herself on the south side with the river between, and no bridge. One wonders why her 'Voices', which had been so explicit about banners and swords, could not, if they were of divine origin, supply her with some elementary notions of geography. However, it may well be that those who guided her at the court were not with the army and so unable to keep her informed. If so La Trémoille had done a good job of isolating her and keeping her under control.

There were, in fact, good tactical reasons for advancing along the south bank. The bulk of the English forces were concentrated on the south and west of the town. The only gate that was open was in the east, the Burgoyne gate. The intention was to march past the town on the south side, cross the river and enter by this gate. It was a play-safe policy but it did mean that they were not in danger of losing their supplies in a surprise attack. In fact the English watched the French army arrive and did not once show their faces.

When Dunois rode out to meet the relieving army Joan's greeting was sharp:

'Are you the Bastard of Orléans?'
'Yes, I am, and happy that you are here.'
'Was it you who suggested that I should come on this side of the river instead of going straight to where Talbot and the English are?'
'Yes, and others cleverer than I, who gave this advice thinking it would better serve the safety of our enterprise.'

Dunois' last reply gives some idea of the consultations which were taking place behind Joan's back and indicates how limited her rôle was intended to be. The 'others cleverer than I' were doubtless La Trémoille and Gilles. The king's favourite was not going to allow this girl from nowhere to conduct a runaway campaign and eclipse his influence. She was to be kept on a tight rein, and Gilles was there to do it.

Dunois' answer did not satisfy Joan:

In God's name, [she said, as he reported later] My Lord's counsel is clever and safer than yours! You thought you were deceiving me but you have deceived yourselves even more, for

I bring you better help than any captain or any town ever had, the help of the King of Heaven. This help has not come for my sake, but from God himself, who has heard the prayers of Saint Louis and Saint Charlemagne, and will not suffer the enemy to possess both the body of the Duke of Orléans and his town.

This was the first of many such bitter exchanges, and always for the same reason: a clash between Joan's impatience to pass straight over to the attack and the more traditionally cautious attitudes of the French commanders. For the moment Gilles was at one with his fellow captains.

As though to mark Joan's point about the route that had been taken, the wind turned blustery and unfavourable so that the troops and supplies could not be carried to the other side, and the level of the water proved to be too low to support the heavy barges they intended using. The army was stranded on the south bank. Suddenly the wind changed and the level of the water rose so that the crossing was made possible. Both events were later regarded as miraculous.

In fact, for once, the French commanders had taken a much more realistic view of the situation than she had. Her plan was naïve. She intended marching straight to the English positions, delivering an ultimatum, which was a follow-up to the one she had already sent on March 22, and attacking if it was not accepted. This was to ignore the complexity of the situation in which she found herself. Gilles, Dunois and the other commanders realised that the food supplies they had brought with them would not be sufficient to feed the townspeople and the army and that more would be needed. Moreover troops were still being levied in Blois and would have to be brought over if the army was to be at full strength before the attack. After some discussion it was decided that Gilles and De Loré should return to Blois to ask for more supplies and marshal the remaining forces, while Dunois and Joan entered Orléans. This was a logical arrangement. Officially Gilles was in charge of the relieving army while Dunois commanded the town garrison. Besides, Joan had an important psychological task to fulfil, to show herself to the townsfolk, who had been expecting her arrival for weeks. Evidently some anxiety was felt about the entry into the town : 'And there concluded all together that she should not enter Orléans before night-time, to avoid the tumult of the people. . . .' Or perhaps it was felt that an entry by torchlight, like the entry at Chinon, would be more theatrically effective.

So on Friday, April 29, Gilles and Ambroise de Loré rode westwards towards Blois while Joan made her triumphal entry into the town at eight in the evening. Gilles must have regretted not being present on this dramatic occasion.

> She entered, armed at all points, riding on a white horse, her standard borne before her, which likewise was white and upon which were two angels each holding a fleur-de-lys in his hand and on the pennon was painted an Annunciation scene. . . .

The populace rushed out to meet her, lighting her way with burning torches and acclaiming her 'as though they had seen God Himself come down among them'.

One small incident almost marred the ceremony. The crowd packed so tightly round her that one of the torches set the pennon on fire. Joan quickly rode up and extinguished it 'as if she had long served in the wars: the which the men-at-arms considered a great marvel and the citizens of Orléans likewise, who bore her company the whole length of the town and city.' Having invested her with magic qualities, they endowed even simple presence of mind with miraculous overtones.

The next day, the 30th, Joan went to see Dunois who again refused to engage the enemy until Gilles had returned with reinforcements. She did not disguise her anger at this decision but she was powerless to do anything about it. She made a tour of the English fortifications, calling on them to surrender and being called 'cow-girl', 'bitch' and 'whore' for her pains.

Once he had arrived in Blois Gilles explained the situation 'to my Lord Chancellor and other members of the King's council who were there present [and] they ordered a great quantity of food to be gathered, which was done with all speed, and decided that it should be taken by the Beauce route [i.e. North of the Loire]'.

The change of route is interesting and may have been influenced by two factors; first the fact that the English army had not reacted in any way to the arrival of French reinforcements, second the difficulty that had been experienced in transporting supplies across the river. Another possible factor is the beginning of a change in Gilles' attitude. However much he might agree in principle with the wisdom of his fellow commanders' decisions, however willing he might be to serve his cousin, his instincts urged him to side with Joan. Both were impatient, both believed in a fight to the finish, both were all-or-nothing characters. And if she was willing to march along the north bank why shouldn't he? He was not the sort of person to be outdone.

On Sunday, May 1, which was, as usual, a day of truce, Dunois rode out to meet Gilles and the column of supplies and reinforcements. There does not appear to have been any special reason for this. Joan was left behind, still obliged to play her rôle as talisman and magical symbol. She showed herself to the townsfolk and made another tour of the English fortifications where, once more, she was insulted and abused. She did the same on Monday. On Tuesday there was a torchlight procession and finally on Wednesday news came that the reinforcements, headed by Gilles and Dunois, had been sighted.

On Wednesday, 4th day of this month of May, the Maid sallied forth into the fields ... and went to meet the Bastard of Orléans, the Marshal [sic] de Rais, the Marshals de Sainct Sévère, the Baron de Coulonces and many other knights and squires ... who brought foodstuffs that the people of Bourges, Angers, Tours and Blois sent to the people of Orléans and who were received with great joy in the town, which they entered passing before the fortifications of the English who dared not come forth but kept within their defences.

Dunois went to Joan's lodging that same afternoon and told her that an enemy captain, John Falstaff, was reported to be on his way with fresh troops and supplies to support the besieging army. Joan told him to be sure to let her know of the Englishman's arrival, otherwise she would have his head. In the words of her squire, Jean d'Aulon:

I then being exhausted and weary lay me down upon a mattress in the Maid's room. And Joan also lay her down to

rest on another bed, with her hostess. But as I was about to
fall asleep the Maid sprang up from her bed making a great
noise and woke me.

Her 'Voices' had apparently told her to go out against the
English, but they had not told her where. Did they mean her to
go to the ramparts, or to leave the town and intercept Falstaff
and his supply train? She ran downstairs to her page, calling
him 'bloody boy' for not telling her there was fighting going on.
While he ran to saddle her horse she was helped into her armour
by the hostess and her daughter. She sent another page, Louis de
Contes, upstairs to fetch the banner she had left there. It was
handed to her through the window after she had mounted. She
then rode towards the Burgoyne gate where she could see smoke
and flames and hear the sound of fighting.

The action was completely unplanned. Some over-enthusiastic
citizens, fired by her presence, had attempted a sortie of their
own against the English, and had been pushed back by a
vigorous English counter-attack. Joan wept when she saw the
number of dead and wounded. She then took command and
rode out against the English fortification at Saint-Loup. This
was not a wise move. Talbot immediately sent out troops from
the other forts to attack the French in the rear. Joan was thus
caught between two fires. Lookouts on the city ramparts saw
what was happening and raised the alarm by ringing the church
bells. Gilles immediately called his troops together and with
La Hire at his side rode out to the rescue. The English in their
turn found themselves attacked from the rear and were obliged
to retreat. The combined French forces then attacked the fortification of Saint-Loup, which the English had not had time
to secure properly, and took it. It was the first victory of the
campaign; it might well have been the first disaster.

A great deal has been written since about Joan's innate
military skill but certainly on this occasion it was not in evidence.
Had it not been for Gilles' almost classic rescue she might have
been killed or captured there and then, and the blow to French
morale would have been incalculable. Her 'Voices' had given
her very imprecise information as to what she was to do and
she quite obviously lost her head in the heat of the moment.

None the less it may well have been incidents such as these, where victory was snatched from apparent disaster, which persuaded the English, who were as superstitious as their opponents, that they were dealing with the supernatural. Certainly the sight of a woman dressed in white armour, carrying a white banner and leading troops into battle, must have been impressive, whatever abuse they might throw at her. Besides her frequent trips to the fortifications, her summons to the English to surrender must have taken on a magic aura, as though she was trying to put a spell on them, or conjure them to surrender.

The following day, Thursday, Ascension Day, Joan sent another letter to the English, which she shot on the end of an arrow. The only answer she received was to be called a whore again. This time she was reduced to tears. On the same day Gilles and Dunois held a council of war at the house of Jacques Boucher. Although this was the house she was lodged in, Joan was specifically not invited. This must have been a direct consequence of the previous day's events. Two possible attacks were discussed against English positions south of the river: the first against the fort of Saint-Jean-le-Blanc, the second against the fort of Les Augustins which served as first line of defence for Les Tourelles. Both ideas were rejected. It was decided that there would be no attack on the following day, and orders were given for the city gates to be barred and bolted to prevent any wild sorties on the previous days' patterns.

Gaucourt, one of the leading exponents of a play-safe policy, informed Joan of the council's decision. She turned on him angrily, calling him a wicked man and saying, 'The soldiers will break out whether you like it or not and they will win, just as they have won elsewhere.' The only other place they had won was Saint-Loup on the previous day. It was evident that Joan was not put off by the near disaster and was ready to repeat the experiment. As Jean Chartier states:

> And very often the said Bastard and the other captains came together to take counsel as to what was to be done and whatever conclusion they came to when this same Joan the Maid arrived, she decided quite another thing, against the opinions of all the captains, war chiefs and others, and made fine sorties against the enemy, which always had good results.

Where did Gilles stand in all these arguments? Unfortunately we have everybody's testimony but his own. At the Rehabilitation trial of 1456 everyone gave his own version and everyone was careful not to mention Gilles' name. The memory of his disgrace was far too recent for that. In fact, apart from a passing reference made by Dunois, it might be concluded that he was not there at all. It is only by piecing together odd references in various chronicles that we can obtain any information as to his activities at all. What we do know is that when Joan acted entirely on her own initiative he was the first to help her.

On May 6 Joan crossed the river to attack the English positions on the south bank. She had with her a mere handful of troops most of whom were inexperienced. 'And against the will of my lord de Gaucourt, the soldiers who were in the town made an attack against the bastion of Les Augustins.'

The original intention had been to attack Saint-Jean-le-Blanc but the English retired to the greater safety of Les Augustins when they saw the French forces approaching. Faced with the prospect of attacking a much more strongly fortified position, French confidence failed and they started to withdraw. Once more it appears to have been Gilles, watching from the north bank, who saved the day. According to Jean Chartier, 'the Maid placed her standard before the fortress of Les Augustins, where came straightway the Sire de Rais'.

This was the signal for others to follow suit, despite the decisions of the Council of War the previous day. 'And the French continually grew in numbers, so that they took the fortress of the said Augustins, where the English were in great number, all of whom were straightaway killed.'

Logically the next step was to take the fortress of Les Tourelles, which was a key point in the disposition of the English forces. If the French could take it they would control the river once more and could cross with fresh troops and supplies at will. Joan decided to press her advantage and immediately laid siege to it. De Gaucourt was against this, arguing that there was sufficient food in the town and that all they need do was await further help from the king. It is difficult to see what more he expected. Every last penny had been spent; Charles was unlikely to provide more than he had already. Joan rejected these arguments, and prepared for an attack the next day. The army spent the night in the open, 'for which reason the people of Orléans were most diligent in bringing all through the night bread, wine and other food to the men-at-arms who were maintaining the siege'.

We have no record of any conversation which took place nor any revealing incident which occurred, but it must have been about this time that the friendship between Gilles and Joan of Arc began to develop. Gilles' sudden move across the river to go to her support indicated, perhaps without his realising it, his commitment to her views and her tactics. They had much in common: both were reckless in battle; they both preferred a simple response to any situation; they both had a sense of occasion, of the theatrical; and they both shared a fondness for fine clothes. Gilles had never really understood the tortuous machinations of his grandfather and his cousin. He had simply gone along. Joan's very simpleness and directness appealed to him. For her part she had every reason to be grateful to him. He had saved her twice; she could turn to him in a difficult situation; she could, in her own way, exploit him. Perhaps even more important to Gilles was the magical world in which Joan lived, half heaven, half earth. When he rode and fought with her he became part of a living legend, a world of romance and literature come to life. He had been brought up to think of himself as a little emperor; now his kingdom had a celestial glow around it.

On Saturday, May 7, Jean Pasquerel said an early Mass and the assault began. It lasted all day until sunset. Joan herself was wounded during the course of the morning. The French troops attacked boldly, attempting to scale the walls. Joan was hit in the shoulder by an arrow from a crossbow while trying to place a ladder against the fortifications. Gilles caught her and removed her to a safe distance. He helped take off her armour so that the wound could be dressed. One of the soldiers wanted to 'charm' it, but she refused. She was convinced that she would not die until her mission was completed. A simple dressing of lard and olive oil was applied. Joan then returned, with Gilles, to the fight.

When no progress had been made by sunset Dunois and several of the others were prepared to abandon the attack and retire to the town. Joan asked them to wait. She then withdrew for a while into a vineyard, leaving her standard near the English defences. Then another 'miraculous' incident occurred. Joan called out to one of the gentlemen: ' "Watch and see when the tip of my standard touches the English defences." And a short while after he said, "Joan, the tip is touching." And then she answered him, "All is yours! Enter the fort!" ' It was moments like these which inspired the French army without exception.

The townspeople, who had been watching from the other side of the river, poured out of the town across the bridge when they realised the army meant to continue to fight. They replaced the broken arches with an improvised structure made from ladders and pieces of wooden guttering, finally completed with an odd plank. The troops who had stayed in the town were thus able to cross the river and attack the fortress from the other side.

English resistance suddenly collapsed and they attempted to retreat across the newly repaired bridge. Unfortunately for them the local fishermen had anticipated their move. They floated a flaming barge downstream. It lodged against the makeshift woodwork. Within minutes the bridge gave way and the bulk of the English forces, including their commander, Glasdale, were drowned. While Joan shed tears of compassion for them the townsfolk merely regretted the loss of so much good ransom money.

On Sunday, May 8, the English left their fortresses and ranged themselves in battle order. Joan then rode out with Gilles, the other commanders, and all her forces and drew up against them. As it was the sabbath she forbade her troops to attack unless provoked. The two armies stood looking at each other for an hour, then the English turned away and rode off in orderly fashion towards Melun. The siege of Orléans was over.

5

Coronation

ON THE EVENING of May 8 there were celebrations in the town. They continued into the following day. The army paraded through the town with the clergy at its head, going from church to church. Prominent among the commanders was Gilles himself, who was recognised by the townsfolk as one of the heroes of the campaign. When, some years later, the municipal authorities decided to hold annual celebrations in honour of their delivery they bought the banner 'which had belonged to Monseigneur de Rais to show in what manner Les Tourelles was taken from the English'. There was no doubt in their minds at that date as to where their gratitude should lie.

On the 9th, after a short rest 'departed ... the Maid and with her my lord de Rais, the baron de Coulonces and several other knights, squires and men-at-arms and went to the king, to take him the news of the noble work that had been done, and also to prepare him to be crowned and consecrated at Reims as our Lord had commanded'.

This provoked a fresh series of arguments. Joan was quite clear in her own mind as to what the order of events should be; she had an established time-table. First Orléans was to be delivered, then the coronation was to take place with the minimum of delay. Previously she had been anxious to fight; now her mind was fixed on the ceremony at Reims. The king was undecided. La Trémoille was still anxious to keep the Maid in check, and perhaps none too pleased with his young cousin who was beginning to forget why he had been appointed.

The king held a succession of meetings in which various plans were discussed. One scheme was to invade Normandy, another, far the more practical, was to follow up the success at Orléans by consolidating the whole of the Loire valley. The wrangling went on for a month. Joan was excluded but she appears to have been kept informed of all discussions that took place, probably by those guiding her, and her constant answer was that the coronation should take place without delay. The more the king prevaricated the more she insisted. For someone who was acknowledged to be receiving her instructions from heaven she had a remarkably difficult time in making her point.

Why was she so adamant? Because she only dealt basically in symbolic acts. The raising of the siege of Orléans had been a symbol. It represented the revival of French hopes and confidence. They had won their first victory in living memory. Now a religious and psychologically effective ritual was needed. Young Henry VI of England had not yet been crowned king of France. Charles' coronation would end all doubts as to his parentage and right to succeed. Once consecrated, in the people's eyes, and his own, he would be the rightful king.

If Joan insisted that the ceremony should take place at once in Reims, rather than wait until Paris was liberated, it was because the holy oil, which according to legend had been used to anoint every French king since Clovis, was kept in the nearby Abbey of Saint-Rémy. The fact that the Archbishop of Reims, Regnault de Chartres, was actively hostile to her did not deter her at all.

Charles finally decided to have it both ways. He agreed to go to Reims for the coronation, but while preparations for it were being made, he would campaign in the Loire valley.

In fact, during Joan's absence at court, Dunois and those commanders who had stayed behind in Orléans had made preliminary sorties against the nearby town of Jargeau, but had found the moat impassable. It was therefore decided that the first move in the campaign would be to mount a full-scale attack.

It was at this moment that Gilles suffered a slight eclipse. It coincided with the re-emergence of the Duc d'Alençon. D'Alencon had been taken prisoner at Verneuil in 1425. Part of his ransom had been paid and he had been released. However, under the code of mediaeval chivalry, he could not undertake active service until the full amount had been paid. By selling off some of his estates he was able to make himself eligible to fight immediately after the victory at Orléans. He was immediately created Lieutenant-General of the king's army, with full powers of command.

It is inconceivable that this appointment should have been made without La Trémoille's approval. Apart from giving d'Alençon a position commensurate with his rank, this may have been La Trémoille's way of separating his cousin from Joan. If they both held positions of absolute authority any hope of controlling them might be lost. Perhaps d'Alençon might be less impressionable.

La Trémoille had no wish to loose Gilles' support altogether. It was at this moment that he told him, unofficially, that he was to be made Marshal of France. This was a position that gave more honour than power, but it was sufficient to flatter Gilles and gave him even more opportunity for display.

On June 9, one month after leaving it, Joan and her forces made a triumphal entry into Orléans. Gilles' name curiously disappears from the account given by the *Journal du Siège d'Orléans,* which is normally scrupulous in recording the notables present on any given occasion. Neither is he mentioned in the account of the battle of Jargeau. However the following document from the royal treasury exists:

> To Messire Gilles de Rais, counsellor and chamberlain to our lord the king, Marshal of France [*sic*] the sum of 1,000 livres that the king our said lord, by his letters patent given the 21 June 1429, has ordered to be given to him, something to recompense him for the great expense he has made in order that he might raise and assemble, at the king's command, a great company of men-at-arms and artillery, and for having used them in his service in the company of Joan the Maid, so as to bring the town of Jargeau, held by the English, back into submission to the king.

La Trémoille was not in the habit of paying out money for nothing, so we may assume that when the royal army moved out of Orléans on Saturday, June 11, Gilles was in his rightful place beside the other captains. With them were 8,000 horse and foot and a large amount of artillery. The English garrison, under the command of the Earl of Suffolk, William de la Pole, numbered about 700 or 800 men. They, too, were well equipped with artillery.

The French assault met strong resistance and once again was almost destroyed by lack of co-ordination. News came that a convoy of provisions, artillery and 2,000 reinforcements was on its way to relieve Suffolk and his men. One section of the army was in favour of attacking the supply train immediately, but this would have seriously reduced the force of the French attack, 'and in fact many rode off, and all the others would have done likewise had not the Maid and many lords and captains been there, who by their fine words caused them to remain and called back the others; so that the siege was continued. . . .'

There can be little doubt which strategy Gilles would have favoured: a brutal frontal assault pursued to the bitter end before reinforcements could arrive. He had shown the kind of attack he favoured at Lude.

The following day, the 12th, the walls were scaled. The English attempted a retreat. De la Pole and his brother John were captured; Alexander de la Pole, his other brother, was killed. The whole town, including the church, was pillaged.

The army then returned to Orléans where they waited a short while so that more troops could join them. The king, whose life was a succession of journeys from one place to another, took up residence at Sully-sur-Loire. If the army expected him to join them in Orléans they were disappointed. La Trémoille held him back.

On June 15 the army set out from Orléans in the direction of Beaugency. They captured the bridge at Meung-sur-Loire, which was heavily defended, en route, 'by frontal assault, hardly causing a moment's pause'. On the following day the French army entered the town of Beaugency without a struggle. The English had already retreated to the safety of the castle, which commanded the bridge over the Loire, also heavily fortified. A few English troops had been left behind in the town itself and they harassed the French troops as they began to settle in. However, after some minor skirmishing these, too, joined the main body of their forces in the castle. The French then brought up their artillery and prepared to launch the preliminary bombardment.

It was at this moment that Arthur de Richemont arrived. He offered to throw the full support of his troops behind the attack.

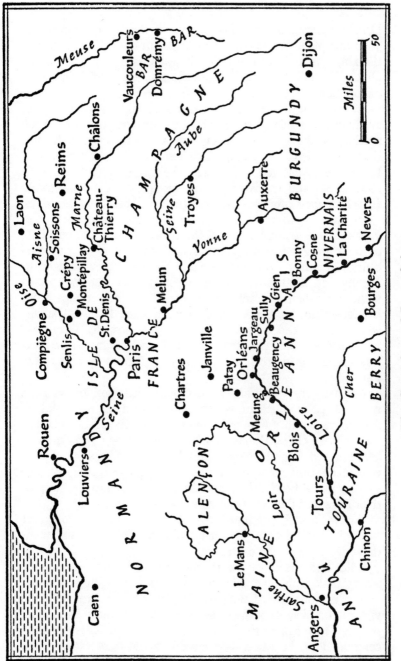

The Campaigns of Joan of Arc

Despite opposition from d'Alençon and the other commanders Joan accepted, first making him swear an oath of allegiance to the king. As a political decision it was disastrous; it confirmed all La Trémoille's suspicions that she was a potential danger to his position.

It was agreed that de Richemont should attack from the southern side while Joan and her companions attacked from the north. As they were drawing up their forces the English commander asked to parley. As a result of the negotiations the English were allowed to evacuate the castle at midnight with their horses and goods not exceeding the value of one mark. In return they promised not to fight for a period of ten days.

In the meantime an English army under Talbot and John Falstaff were marching south from Paris. They left the bulk of their provisions and cannons at Estampes so as to travel quickly. Finding Beaugency already occupied, they went on to Meung and tried to recapture the bridge but were obliged to withdraw when an advance party of French troops from Beaugency set on them. They then marched towards Janville which they intended to fortify and hold if possible. They were forestalled by a detachment of the French army which now was advancing in good order, and obliged to set up camp near Patay.

Normally they would have surrounded their position with the rows of pointed stakes which had proved so successful at Agincourt, but they were not given the time. The French cavalry, led by Joan, Gilles, Dunois and Xantrailles, rode down on them, killing 2,500 English soldiers and French collaborators. Talbot was taken prisoner and Falstaff fled. The retreating English soldiers made for Janville, but the townsfolk shut the gates in their faces and then surrendered to the royal troops.

While Falstaff continued to retreat the English forces at Montpipeau and Saint-Sigismond burned their forts and withdrew. By June 18 the campaign was over.

Gilles and the other commanders could be forgiven if they were drunk with their own success and filled with a religious or superstitious awe of this peasant girl who had brought them victory. In nine days they had reversed the whole balance of power. There can be no doubt that by this time Gilles was fully committed to the Maid. She gave him the most exciting, the most fulfilled period in his life. What at other times might have been criminal was sanctified by God and surrounded with glory.

The French army rode back to Orléans on the 19th in exultant mood. They fully expected the king to join them there and prepared a great welcome. But Charles did not come; La Trémoille would not let him. He stayed at Sully-sur-Loire. The townsfolk were a little put out and bewildered. Joan went to meet the king, who had moved again, at Saint-Benoît-sur-Loire. She again tried to persuade him to take de Richemont back into favour. Whoever urged her to do this, possibly Yolande d'Aragon, or her 'Voices', must have been aware of the risks involved. The king half gave his consent but withdrew it after he had consulted La Trémoille.

The court and the army finally met at Gien on June 24. More discussions followed. Joan was insistent that the coronation should have absolute priority. Others argued that it would be better to take Cosne and La Charité first, and thus ensure control of the whole Loire valley.

Charles finally made up his mind to follow Joan's advice and on June 29 left Gien for Reims, attended by the court and the army. The journey would take them through territory largely held by Burgundian forces. After two days they reached Auxerre. Joan and Gilles, supported by the other commanders, were for making an immediate assault but La Trémoille had other ideas. He negotiated with the town authorities and it was agreed that the town would be spared in return for payment of 2,000 *écus* and an ample supply of provisions. Apart from the question of personal gain La Trémoille was thus able to prevent another spectacular success to enhance Joan's reputation. Auxerre surrendered on July 1.

Saint Florentin surrendered immediately after and the army marched on towards Troyes. On July 4 Joan sent a letter demanding immediate surrender but the answer she received was one of defiance. The army set up camp outside the walls. Morale was low. They had no money, they had no food. Some 5–6,000 men spent a week out in the open without bread, and only the fact that the surrounding fields had been sown with a crop of beans prevented them from dying of starvation. The situation was so dispiriting that many encouraged the king to return to Orléans at once. Even if Troyes could be brought to heel, Châlons and Reims itself were still in enemy hands. An army which was unpaid and unfed could not go on fighting. The Archbishop of Reims, Regnault de Chartres, was all for turning back, mainly because he did not wish to perform the coronation ceremony. Joan insisted that the town would surrender within two days.

Despite all the doubts that were current the siege was prepared; brushwood was collected to fill the moat and the artillery was put in position. However, there was a pro-French faction in the town, led by Brother Richard, a friar who had been expelled from Paris for preaching anti-English sermons. He was in favour of surrender but he was uncertain as to Joan's true nature. He suspected that she was a witch. He came out to meet her, sprinkling a great deal of holy water and crossing himself frequently. Joan laughed at him and said, 'Walk up boldly. I shan't fly away.' In view of the witch-cult theory both his doubts and her answer are significant. They reached an agreement, and the town surrendered on July 10. The Anglo-Burgundian garrison evacuated the town without a fight on the same day.

The royal army continued its journey. On July 14 the Bishop of Châlons came out to meet them and formally declared the town's allegiance and they moved on towards Reims. Joan was confident it, too, would surrender, and in this she was right. The Anglo-Burgundian garrison did not feel strong enough to resist the full force of the French army. They told the townspeople to hold out for six weeks by which time they would return with reinforcements. Then they left.

News now reached the town that Châlons had surrendered, and the citizens of Troyes sent a letter stating that they, too, had gone over to Charles' side. In return for a general amnesty the citizens of Reims surrendered the town to the king on July 16.

Regnault de Chartres, the Archbishop, who had never set foot inside the town since his appointment, prepared to crown Charles on the following morning.

The coronation was in many respects a makeshift affair but, together with the victory at Orléans, represents the peak of Gilles' career at court. He was given a prominent rôle in the ceremonies. Neither the Queen nor her mother was present.

They had been sent back to Bourges, where they would be safer. Three gentlemen from Anjou wrote to Yolande d'Aragon giving her a fairly exact description of the day's events and of the part Gilles played in them. The ceremony was performed on Sunday July 17 and lasted from nine in the morning until two in the afternoon. One of the most important tasks was to go and fetch the sacred oil from the Abbey of Saint-Rémy. The letter states:

> To go and fetch the holy ampulla from the Abbey of Saint-Rémy and to bring it to the church of Notre Dame, where the ceremony took place, were appointed the Marshal de Boussac, my lords de Rais and Oraville and the Admiral (Culan) with their four banners, which each carried in his hand, armed at all points and on horseback and with a fitting retinue. And they fetched the Abbot from the said place, who bore the ampulla. And they entered the great church on horseback and dismounted at the entrance to the choir. And they returned the ampulla to the said abbey in like manner after the service. Which service lasted from nine until two. And at the moment when the king was anointed and the crown was placed on his head, every man cried 'Noel' and the trumpets sounded in such a manner that they almost lifted the roof off the church.

More honours awaited Gilles that day. He was officially created Marshal of France at the exceptional age of twenty-five. Joan wept for joy and Gilles was the most favoured man at court, but the epic period was over. Now the chicanery began in earnest.

6

The Siege of Paris

GILLES, DUNOIS, D'ALENÇON and the other commanders were now prepared to embark on any campaign Joan cared to suggest, but as far as the king was concerned the war was over, for the time being, at least. Charles was tired; he wanted to retire south of the Loire to security and peace. La Trémoille encouraged him in this. While he could not come out openly against a national heroine, since she had made the mistake of pleading for de Richemont, he employed every backstairs manoeuvre available to undermine her influence and sabotage her plans.

She still had a function to perform, which was to be seen at parades and triumphal entries. She was raised to the nobility, Joan the Maid becoming Joan of Arc; she was shown every respect. As town after town hastened to declare its allegiance to the new king she was to be seen with Charles, Gilles and the other captains in a glittering cortège, but she was not allowed to do what she really wanted.

La Trémoille in the meantime was negotiating with the Duke of Burgundy, in an attempt to gain by diplomacy what Joan wanted to win by battle. His object was to draw Burgundy away from the English alliance by persuading him that the tide had definitely turned in Charles' favour.

When an initial truce of fifteen days was agreed Joan made no attempt to conceal her anger. She wrote to the citizens of Reims, 'I am not pleased and do not know if I will keep it. But if I do, it will only be to preserve the king's honour.'

For the first time she was speaking in her own accent, without guidance. Her 'Voices' had suddenly stopped giving her instructions, but she persisted. Perhaps she was beginning to believe her own legend. Certainly her failure to understand the changed political situation finally cost her her life. This complete blindness to anything except her own desires and schemes she shared with Gilles, who fully supported her in her insistence that the campaign should be continued. His treaty with La Trémoille assumed less and less meaning beside his search for adventure and the pleasures of bloodshed. Two alternative plans of action were suggested. D'Alençon again suggested the recapture of Normandy, while Joan herself favoured a direct assault on Paris.

La Trémoille was entirely opposed to this. If his negotiations with the Duke of Burgundy were successful Paris would fall into Charles' hands without a fight at all. If, on the other hand, Joan were to succeed in recapturing the capital any hope of controlling her would be swept away. He tried to delay all decisions as long as possible.

On July 21 the royal train left Reims. Entering Vailly on the 22nd, Soissons on the 23rd, Laon the day after; then Château-Thierry, Crécy-en-Brie and Provins in quick succession, Compiègne was undecided but willing to negotiate.

The English on their side were in no doubt as to what the next move would be. They anticipated an immediate attack on Paris. Large numbers of people evacuated the city together with their belongings. Even the Duchess of Bedford took refuge with her brother Philippe le Bon. Bedford himself left Paris with his army of some ten thousand men and marched south in an attempt to stave off the attack, then suddenly changed his mind and returned to the capital. Charles on his side, prompted by La Trémoille, decided to return to safer ground.

The two armies were avoiding each other and this did not please Gilles and the other French commanders. It seemed absurd to withdraw at the very moment when the English, whose army was no smaller than their own, were obviously unwilling to fight. Their protests were loud enough to make Charles change his mind once more and return to Château-Thierry. From there he moved to Crépy-en-Valois, after which a further short march brought him to Dampmartin-en-Gouelle where he received the dutiful submission of more citizens who came out to meet him shouting 'Noël' and singing the Te Deum.

Bedford left Paris once more and made camp near the French army. He then drew up his troops in battle order and waited. Charles followed suit. Apart from light skirmishing, nothing happened. Bedford withdrew once more to Paris and Charles to Crépy-en-Valois. Royal heralds were despatched to Compiègne, whose citizens were still prevaricating, to call them to their true allegiance. They surrendered immediately.

This shadow boxing while La Trémoille negotiated with the Duke of Burgundy did not suit Joan and her companions. The French army had fallen back into its old ways, more concerned with forms than with victory. Bedford, on his side, was waiting for reinforcements, but he was astute enough to hand over control of Paris to the Burgundian army, so that if the French should attack they would be brought into direct conflict with the very man with whom they were negotiating.

A few days later it seemed as though the battle the French commanders had been waiting for might finally take place. Bedford marched out of Paris again, with the 4,000 reinforcements he had been waiting for, and moved towards Senlis. When the news of this move reached Compiègne, Charles was prevailed upon to march to Barron, a village some two leagues from Senlis, and set up camp. De Loré and Xantrailles were sent to reconnoitre. They found that in order to reach Senlis the English would have to cross the River Nonette. The ford was so narrow that they would have to pass across in double file, which meant that they would be strung out and vulnerable. De Loré and Xantrailles sent word to the king that he should immediately mount an ambush, but he delayed, and by the time the French forces arrived the bulk of the English army was already across and the opportune moment had passed.

The two armies took up positions in sight of one another; the English near the river-bank, the French near Montépillay. Mild skirmishing took place but no serious engagement occurred. The English set up their defences during the night, surrounding themselves with their traditional pointed stakes.

The next morning the French drew up in battle formation. The main part of the army was divided into three groups; the vanguard led by d'Alençon, the centre by René Anjou and the rearguard by the king himself. The flanks were protected by Gilles on the one side and Sainte-Sévère on the other. A separate force was placed under the command of Joan, Dunois and La Hire. This had greater freedom of action and was to be responsible for harassing the enemy.

On the surface this seems a reasonable disposition of forces, for which, officially at least, the king was responsible. But it is worth noting how the really effective commanders, Joan, Gilles, d'Alençon and Sainte-Sévère, were separated from each other; Joan herself was virtually consigned to the periphery of the battle. There was to be no concerted effort as there had been at Orléans, no spectacular victory for the Maid and her companions. It is difficult not to conclude, particularly in view of his later conduct, that La Trémoille was responsible.

The English continued to fortify their positions. Charles himself rode out to inspect the situation, and his own observation, confirmed by the reports from the spies who had been sent out, made it clear that a frontal assault would cause very heavy losses. Nonetheless he brought the army to within two crossbow shots of the English army and waited for them to come out and fight.

The English were not willing to risk a pitched battle however. Joan herself engaged in skirmishing throughout the day while Gilles was obliged to look impotently on. La Trémoille then decided to ride out into the no-man's-land between the two armies and join in what fighting there was. It was a foolish move. Perhaps he wanted to show that he, too, was capable of leading an army, or that his decision to hold back was not based on personal cowardice. Unfortunately for him he was neither the horseman nor the soldier he thought he was. His horse stumbled and he was thrown right into the middle of a group of English soldiers. He had to be rescued and carried back to the French lines. Skirmishing continued until nightfall and, to judge from contemporary accounts, everyone seems to have enjoyed themselves. The traditional war-game had been re-established without there being any danger of a decisive victory for either side.

At dusk the English retired to their positions and the French to theirs. The next morning Bedford withdrew to Paris and Charles to Crépy-en-Valois, where he spent the night, riding on to Compiègne the following day. In August he acknowledged the submission of the citizens of Beauvais, Senlis, Creil and Point-Sainte-Maxence. He had had enough. His only thought was to go back to a quiet life in the Loire valley and forget all about fighting.

There was widespread discontent in the army. Joan, acting

now entirely on her own initiative, without the benefit of advice from her 'Voices', insisted that she should be allowed to attack Paris. D'Alençon backed her and pleaded with the king that, since the English had shown quite clearly they were afraid to fight, this was the moment to follow up an advantage. Not only Paris was vulnerable but the whole of Normandy as well. Bedford was aware of this, too, and had withdrawn the bulk of his forces from the capital and spread them across the Norman plain. Gilles, for his part, left Joan in no doubt that he and his troops would go with her wherever she wished to fight.

La Trémoille, who was still suffering from the effects of his fall, was in a difficult position. He could not oppose Joan openly, although he could circumvent her plans, but he had to tread much more carefully with Dunois, d'Alençon, La Hire and his hot-headed cousin. Accordingly he advised the king to allow Joan to launch an assault against Paris.

On August 23 Joan set out accompanied by d'Alençon and Gilles, whom she had specifically requested should be allowed to accompany her. On the 26th they occupied Saint-Denis, and Paris lay before them. Inside the city itself hasty preparations were made to resist the forthcoming attack; ditches were dug, positions fortified, jewels and church valuables sold off so as to pay the defending troops. On the whole the people of Paris did not give much for their chances.

In the event it was La Trémoille who saved them. While Joan and her companions were preparing their attack he was making sure that it either would never take place or would never reach a successful conclusion. He put the finishing touches to his treaty with the Duke of Burgundy and it was signed on August 28, two days after the capture of Saint-Denis. It made nonsense of everything Joan and Gilles and the other French commanders were trying to achieve.

Under its terms a truce was agreed until December 25. This truce was operative north of the Seine, from Nogent-sur-Seine to Harfleur, but did not apply to the fortified towns along the river itself. That is, it did not apply to Paris. To make certain that there could be no misunderstanding, it was stated, quite specifically, that the Duke of Burgundy had the right to support the English garrison in Paris if the town was attacked by anybody whatsoever.

It was small wonder, then, that d'Alençon had difficulty in persuading the king to join the army at Saint-Denis. Twice he rode to Senlis, leaving Joan in Gilles' care, to try to persuade his royal master to make some show of supporting them. Finally on September 7, an unwilling Charles rode into Saint-Denis. After some preliminary skirmishing the army then prepared their main attack.

And the third day [September 7] the Maid and the Duc d'Alençon, the Duc de Bourbon, the Comte de Vendôme, the Comte de Laval and the Marshals de Sainte-Sévère and de Rais, La Hire, Pothon de Xantrailles and many other valiant knights, captains and squires, together with a great number of valiant men-at-arms, departed and went to lodge in a village called La Chappelle, which is on the way and about mid-way between Saint-Denis and Paris. And the next day arrayed themselves in good order at the Pig-market, before the Saint-Honoré gate, and brought up several cannon, which they fired in divers places, often reaching inside the town itself.

Any hopes that the town might surrender without a prolonged struggle were soon dispelled. A letter d'Alençon sent to the municipal authorities was greeted with derision. He was told 'not to throw his litter about'.

On September 8 an attack was launched. The first ditch was filled with wood and faggots and the forward defences taken. It then occurred to d'Alençon that the Anglo-Burgundian forces might leave the town by another gate and attack the French army from the rear. Consequently he and the Duc de Bourbon used their troops to defend the rearguard. (In fact the English had no intention of leaving the safety of the town.) The result of this manoeuvre was to leave the final assault on the Porte Saint-Honoré to Joan and Gilles.

And so, seeing their [the English] cowardice they decided to push their attack right up to the city walls. And indeed to this end she presented herself, having with her ... a great company of men-at-arms and several lords, among whom was the Marshal de Rais. ...

Unfortunately Joan had not counted on there being a second ditch, considerably deeper than the first. She spent some consider-

99

able time trying to gauge its depth with her lance, thus exposing herself to an English crossbow-man, who shot her in the thigh, shouting 'Whore' as he fired. Gilles, who had kept close behind her, dragged her to safety, and her wound was dressed on the spot now occupied by No 4, Place du Théâtre Français. The wound was not serious and Joan wanted to continue the fight, but the ditch seemed bottomless and the soldiers could not fill it no matter how much brushwood they threw in. Night fell, and Joan decided that they would sleep in the open and attack again at dawn. D'Alençon sent word, begging her to withdraw to a safe position for the hours of darkness and, when she refused, had her removed by force to La Chappelle.

It had been a bad day. Losses had been heavy, morale was low and very little had been gained. Joan, moreover, had committed a serious psychological error; she had launched an attack on the birthday of the Blessed Virgin, a religious holiday and consequently a day of truce. Considering her reputation, it was a crass mistake to make, and some of the magic surrounding her began to fade.

That evening the king sent word, or rather La Trémoille sent word, that the attack was to be abandoned and the army was to return to Saint-Denis. There was consternation and anger among Gilles and his companions but they decided to comply with the king's wishes as d'Alençon had already devised another plan of attack:

> The Maid and most of the company were very vexed at this but nevertheless obeyed the king's order hoping they might find a way to take Paris from the other side [the south side of the river], crossing the Seine by a bridge which the Duc d'Alençon had had built near Saint Denis. . . . The following Saturday, some of those who had fought before Paris thought that they would go and cross the river early in the morning by this bridge, but could not because the king, who had heard of the Maid's intention and the purpose of the Duc d'Alençon and other men of good will, had had the bridge destroyed during the night. They were thus prevented. . . .*

The order had come from La Trémoille. The bridge which d'Alençon had made was a temporary structure, consisting

---

* Chronicle of Perceval de Cagny.

mainly of boats. The ropes mooring them had quite simply been cut and the whole arrangement allowed to float away down river.

Feeling ran high and Gilles, like a child who has been thwarted in his favourite game, had an angry outburst against his cousin and the king. It did him no good. On September 12, in a symbolic gesture, Joan laid a suit of armour she had taken from an English gentleman on the altar of the church in Saint Denis. On the 13th the court began its long-awaited journey back to the Loire valley. On the 18th, by a fresh agreement with the Duke of Burgundy, Paris was brought within the terms of the earlier truce. La Trémoille could not have more amply demonstrated his complete control of policy. On September 21, the royal army was disbanded at Gien. The campaign was over. Joan was no longer needed.

Honours were distributed, and this ceremonial paying-off was a public indication that no further action was anticipated. Gilles was granted the right to add the royal arms, fleur-de-lys on an azure ground, to his own—a signal honour, also granted at the same time to Joan. The letters patent authorising this are dated from La Trémoille's own château at Sully-sur-Loire, and speak of Gilles' 'High and commendable services', the 'great perils and dangers' he had run 'as at the capture of Lude, and many other brave feats, the raising of the siege which the English formerly laid at Orléans ... and the day of the battle of Patay, where, once the siege was raised, our enemies were discomfited, and since then, the progress we formerly made, both to the town of Reims for our coronation, and elsewhere, beyond the river Seine, to retake many towns belonging to us.' Joan, significantly, is not mentioned once in the document.

There were no further honours Gilles could receive. La Trémoille could claim, with justice, to have paid him well for his services, however ambiguous they might have been at times. His aim was now to disperse all of Joan's friends. D'Alençon asked that he and Joan should be allowed to campaign in Normandy. This suggestion was blocked and d'Alençon retired to his estates. As for Gilles, he disappears from the records for some fifteen months.

7

Death of Jean de Craon

BETWEEN SEPTEMBER 1429 and December 1430 only two events are recorded in Gilles' life and these cannot be dated with any degree of accuracy. The first is the birth of his daughter Marie de Rais, who was born some time in the late autumn; the second is the sale of one of his castles, Blaison.

Gilles had been paying a private army almost continuously since 1427. It must have been a considerable strain on even his resources, and he tended to keep his troops in style. The thousand *livres* which La Trémoille had given him earlier in the year could have been spent in a day. Gilles' wealth, like that of all his contemporaries, consisted of land and property. What he needed, endlessly, was ready money. It was a problem that was to grow more and more acute with the years.

The sale of Blaison caused a furious quarrel between Gilles and his grandfather. Even thirty years later the inhabitants of Champtocé could remember Jean de Craon hurling abuse at his grandson, calling him a dissolute good-for-nothing who would bring ruin on the whole family. He then bought the castle back so that the de Rais inheritance should be intact.

It is hardly likely that Le Trémoille allowed his cousin to idle his time away on his estates. Gilles was wild and hot-headed and if he began to feel bored he might launch out on some enterprise, perhaps with Joan, that would ruin all La Trémoille's carefully laid plans. The wisest thing was to keep him occupied.

La Trémoille's quarrel with Yolande d'Aragon had long been out in the open. Their opposing views on Joan and the abortive attempt to bring de Richemont back into favour had turned disagreement into bitter hatred. Now the war was over La Trémoille intended to use his cousin once more to strengthen his own position. He could thus be kept out of Joan's way and usefully occupied at the same time. He sent him up into Maine, therefore, to occupy Yolande d'Aragon's castle at Sablé and any other properties he could lay hands on.

We are fortunate in possessing a fairly complete, if one-sided, account of the course of events in *Le Jouvencel* of Jean de Bueil. De Bueil and Gilles had fought side by side against the English but as far as court politics were concerned they were in opposing factions. De Bueil was a staunch supporter of Yolande d'Aragon and de Richemont. When the army was disbanded, in late September, he was given charge of Yolande d'Aragon's possessions in Maine, more particularly of Sablé and Château-l'Hermitage. He took up residence at Château-l'Hermitage at about the same time that Gilles, sent by La Trémoille, took possession of Sablé, which had once, at the end of the fourteenth century, belonged to his family. Whether this fact was used as a feeble sort of justification for his action is not certain. As a consequence, at the national level, the only two strong-points in French hands in otherwise enemy-occupied territory were engaged in a bitter private squabble.

One night, early in 1430, Jean de Bueil left his castle on a raiding expedition when he was informed by his spies that a large troop of soldiers had been seen riding towards Château-L'Hermitage from the direction of Sablé. He immediately turned back only to find that Gilles and his men were already at the castle. Hiding his own troops in the neighbouring wood, de Beuil made his way alone to the moat and tried to call to the sentry on the other side. He was sighted almost at once and taken prisoner but not before he had raised the alarm. Gilles' men almost killed him in their fury. Probably only the thought of ransom money saved him. Gilles was not so indifferent to money as he had been some years earlier. According to de Bueil, Gilles words to him were as follows: 'I would you had had the fever, for had you not come we would have taken this place. As it is we must go, for day is breaking.' The words seem mild enough. We must imagine the fury with which they were uttered.

Gilles took his prisoner back to Sablé and locked him in a tower there. De Bueil used his time and the partial view he had of the ramparts to formulate a plan to capture the castle at a later date. Gilles fixed the ransom money, which was paid almost immediately, and de Bueil was freed. He lost little time in putting his plan into operation, for a document dated 26 October 1430 indicates that Sablé was once more in his hands. Gilles however did recapture it at some unspecified time between late 1430 and July 1433.

Gilles had not lost his taste for pure banditry either. He regularly held merchants and travellers to ransom like a common highwayman. Nobody was exempt. He organised an ambush, possibly with the connivance of his grandfather, against Yolande d'Aragon herself. She was riding quietly through her domains in Anjou and was just entering Ancemis, on the Loire, some fifteen miles from Champtocé, when Gilles and his men attacked part of her escort and stole their horses and some of her baggage. Mention of the attack occurs later in legal documents.

While Gilles returned to the pursuits of his youth Joan had been taken prisoner, tried and condemned to death. There is no evidence that Gilles showed the slightest concern for her fate. Whatever grief or pain he may have felt never reached the surface. He busied himself with other pursuits.

We next hear of him at Louviers on 26 December 1430. Much has been made of the fact that Louviers is not far from Rouen where Joan was being held, and it has been suggested that he was contemplating a desperate rescue attempt. Again there is no evidence for this. What he was in fact doing was buying a horse for one of his men, and borrowing the money to do it. He acknowledged that he owed 'to Roland Mauvoisin, his squire, Captain of Princé, the sum of 160 *écus,* for the purchase of a black horse, saddles and bridles, that he promised to his very dear and good friend and squire Michel Machefer, captain of his men at arms and the archers in his company at Louviers'.

We can only speculate on the reasons for this generosity but it does suggest that whatever was occupying Gilles' mind it was not Joan. This brief document also indicates the pattern which Gilles' life was to follow for the next nine years, especially the endless succession of debts and I.O.U.s. From this moment on, his life is a steady decline. Vestiges of his public life still lingered on, but he was never to be at the centre of things again, partly because of circumstances, partly from his own choice.

*   *   *   *

The old dream of establishing relations between Brittany and France persisted. The marriage which Jean de Craon had so carefully arranged between Isabelle de Bretagne and Yolande d'Aragon's son, Louis III d'Anjou, to cement the alliance, had never taken place, probably for two reasons. The first was Arthur de Richemont's defeat at Saint-James-de-Beuvron and the decline of French hopes. The second was Jean V's unwillingness to part with the dowry. At all events he found another husband for his daughter, Guy XIV de Laval, Gilles' kinsman. Relations with the French court had, as a consequence, become strained. But now it became more important than ever for Charles to secure his position on all sides. Joan's successful campaign had led to an armistice with Burgundy. The fact that she herself was a prisoner worried no-one. In fact, from a diplomatic point of view, it was a distinct advantage. Had she been free, she would only have been advocating a fresh campaign which no one, apart from adventurers like Gilles and d'Alençon, wanted. But if, in addition to ensuring Burgundy's neutrality, an alliance with Brittany could be firmly established, the English would be left without allies and their position would be made decidedly difficult. Fresh approaches were made to Jean V.

Champtocé was the venue chosen for the meetings. A preliminary interview took place some time in 1430 at which Arthur de Richemont, his brother the Comte d'Estampes and Yolande d'Aragon or her representatives were present. Champtocé was the logical choice. Jean de Craon was still Lieutenant-General of Anjou, and Gilles had lands both in France and Brittany as well as a formal treaty of alliance with La Trémoille who would have to be brought into the negotiations at some point, however distasteful his presence might be.

A further meeting took place between Jean V and La Trémoille at Champtocé in February 1431. Discussions lasted from the 22nd to the 24th and resulted in an exchange of letters of friendship between the Duke and La Trémoille, and the arrangement of a marriage between Yolande d'Aragon and François de Bretagne, the Duke's son. The marriage, which took place at Nantes on August 20, was Jean de Craon's last contribution to public life.

We hear nothing definite of Gilles again until the following year. In the interim Joan had been burned at the stake on 30 May 1431 and the English, in a desperate attempt to give some authority to their claims, had crowned the young Henry VI in Notre-Dame cathedral. It has been suggested that Gilles still harboured plans for a last-minute rescue of the Maid and that he even contemplated kidnapping King Henry, but there is no evidence of this. It is more likely that he spent part of his time in private raids, holding local merchants up to ransom, and the other part in lavish entertaining, and in performances of music and plays for which he had a passion.

In the summer of 1432 the English laid siege to Lagny which was strategically placed to control the whole of the Lower Marne. Bedford himself arrived with fresh troops to reinforce the attack. Charles, poor as ever, called on the richest of his marshals to levy troops, pay them with his own money and raise the siege. It was to be Orléans all over again but this time without Joan. On August 10 Gilles attacked the besieging English forces with his usual vigour and Bedford was obliged to withdraw. Without Joan there to restrain him Gilles allowed his men to pillage and plunder as they always had before. Gilles had won an important victory that was to bring him almost as much renown as Orléans, but it no longer seemed to interest him. He never showed any taste for full-scale battle again. On his return to Champtocé he found his grandfather preparing for death.

Jean de Craon had lived like a heretic and a bandit but he was determined to die like a model Christian gentleman. He tried to make amends for his past crimes. He gave money to the peasants on his estates and to the Loire bargemen whom he had ill-treated for so long. He requested a simple funeral; his horse and his weapons were not to feature in the ceremony.

There remained the matter of his will. Gilles was his heir, that he could not change, but he had to make some kind of gesture. They had quarrelled bitterly over the sale of Blaison and it was obvious what Gilles' conduct would be in the future. He was already spending more than his estates brought in, but Jean de Craon had no control over the family fortunes. The fortune he had so carefully built up looked as though it was going to be frittered away. To mark his displeasure he left his sword and breastplate, which should have gone to Gilles, to his younger grandson René de la Suze. It was a public gesture which his contemporaries would know how to interpret. He endowed the · hospitals of Champtocé and Louroux with six and seven beds respectively and died on 15 November 1432. He was buried in the Eglise des Cordeliers on November 26.

Part Two
DELIRIUM

8

The Murders

THE YEAR 1433 marks the turning point in Gilles' career. His life changes course abruptly; it seems almost to break in two, leaving us with apparently contradictory halves. Up to that time he had known little but success and honour. Certainly he was at times ungovernable and extravagant, but that was the privilege of his class. Had he continued in the same vein he would not have been remarkable. He would have come down to us as one of the more colourful figures who helped Joan the Maid to set France on the road to unity and independence. Yet within two years of Joan's trial and execution he emerged as a sadistic pervert and child murderer on a mass scale.

He is quite categorical in dating his crimes from this time. At his trial, later, the court alleged that he had begun as early as 1426. The only evidence which they were able to bring forward was the confession of Gilles' page, later bodyservant, Etienne Corrillaut, known as Poitou, but his testimony on this point was based entirely on hearsay. In his own confession Gilles maintained that the first assaults on children occurred 'in the year in which my lord de la Suze [his grandfather] died', i.e. some time between spring 1432 and spring 1433.* There was no reason for him to have lied. It could have made no difference to the outcome.

As always with Gilles we know nothing of his mental processes. While the external events of his life are to a large extent clear and reveal a logical sequence and structure, his inner life and mind seem impenetrably opaque. Apart from his confessions at the trial, which were almost entirely concerned with facts, we have no direct record of a single statement—not a single

* The mediaeval year, like the current fiscal year, was calculated from April 1 to April 1.

letter, merely one or two quotes reported by his henchmen. People who had known him well were careful not to advertise the fact too openly. At the time of the rehabilitation trial of Joan of Arc in 1453 he was not even mentioned, save in a casual aside by d'Alençon. He was effectively 'unpersoned'. Lacking any direct evidence, if we are to understand the change, or apparent change of personality which took place we must examine to what extent it was precipitated by an alteration in his circumstances.

By 1433 the world in which he had moved with such ease and success had collapsed. The process of disintegration had begun two years earlier with the abortive siege of Paris. By the time his grandfather died it was virtually complete. The war was over, for the time being at least. Charles and the court had decided on a period of consolidation and calm. Fresh campaigning was discouraged. With the army disbanded, nobles were expected either to enjoy the pleasures of the court or to retire to their estates. Moreover, the king was beginning to cast a bleak eye on the private feuds and banditry in which Gilles and his grandfather had indulged in the days when the central government was less certain.

He could now no longer count on the support of his patron. La Trémoille fell from power shortly after Jean de Craon's death, hauled out of bed in the middle of the night and arrested. He was lucky enough to escape with his life. Although Gilles had never quarrelled openly with de Richemont, the new Chancellor, he had been known as La Trémoille's man. Moreover his name was too closely connected with Joan, whom everyone was trying to forget, for the moment at least. All Charles wanted him to do was go away, be quiet, and to hold himself in readiness to perform his duties as Marshal as time and policy required.

But if circumstances had changed, Gilles had not. Like a shipwrecked man, he carried his needs with him. Restless activity, killing and violence, coupled with theatrical display, had been the conditions of his existence. He needed to kill. As a member of a military aristocracy he had been able to do so, had been trained for it. His society had a vested interest in his capacity for violence; under certain circumstances it legitimised and honoured it. Up to now he had received constant praise for his savage outbursts, either from his grandfather or from his king. The psychopathic urgency of his private needs had been concealed by the general brutality of military practice. Only once had he stepped outside the conventions when at Lude he ordered the execution of all prisoners and French collaborators. The only objection that had been raised at the time was a complaint about the loss of ransom money. His reckless abandon and appetite for destruction had finally made him Marshal of France. All that was now at an end.

His world had collapsed once before, in 1415, when both his parents died. Then he had been lost and lonely, full of inexplicable feelings of guilt connected with his parents' disappearance and doubts concerning his own worth as a person. But his grandfather had been there to take over, pampering him, making every decision, seducing him with pleasures and excitements. Someone had always been there to make decisions and keep him, to some extent at least, within bounds—his parents, his tutors, his grandfather, Joan, La Trémoille. La Trémoille was in disgrace, his tutors were hostile and the rest were dead. He was left with a brother who was a stranger if not a rival, a wife whom he despised, a daughter whom he ignored and a group of vicious, unscrupulous cousins and hangers-on he had collected during his military campaigns. What he had was twenty-four estates, in six of which he preferred to live, and the freedom to gratify every whim without hindrance. He was finally and irrevocably his own master.

As the world abandoned him so he abandoned it, almost as a retaliation and a punishment, perhaps. Never again could he be induced to take up arms or participate in public life to any degree, or if he did it was the merest gesture. Just as he appears to have written off Joan after her arrest, so he wrote off everything that he had known. He had the capacity to expunge anything or anyone who had deserted or failed him. For the last seven years of his lfe he lived in a private fantasy, losing contact more and more with reality. From this time on his life seems to fold back on itself. The elements of his past are broken down and reconstituted in a new pattern, are formed into an ideal drama of which he is the central actor. The inadequacies of the real world would be compensated for by the world he would create, and his immense wealth was the magical instrument he would use for this purpose. His world must be shaped to his own desires; unwelcome reality must be blotted out in any way which money could buy. The private universe he created was like a piece of writing, a passage of biographical prose in which he set out his mind.

He wanted above all to recreate the privileged world of his childhood, where gratification was immediate, and everyone around him was a servant. His cousins soon realised that this was the condition of their staying with him. But, paradoxically, it was against children that he turned his murderous instincts and satisfied his need to kill. His victims were small, beautiful children, often fair-haired and fair-skinned, like himself.

*   *   *   *

The first murders occurred at Champtocé where he was living at the time of his grandfather's death. No account of these survives. Shortly after, however, he moved to Machecoul 'in which place', the record of his confession states, 'many children and in great number—which number is uncertain—were killed by him, or at his command, and he committed with them the crime of sodomy, against nature'.

The evidence which we have is in all probability only the tip of the iceberg. We have only five accounts of children disappearing from Machecoul, yet some forty bodies were recovered there in 1437. We must add to these the forty which were removed from Champtocé and which are totally undocumented. This is the reason why some estimates of the number of victims exceeded three hundred.

There were, in addition, huge bands of refugee children, made homeless by a hundred years of war, wandering across the countryside, begging for food where they could. It would not be difficult to lure them in with the promise of a good meal and a warm fire. No one would miss them. No one would complain.

The direct evidence which has come down to us is restricted to Brittany where the official enquiry took place. There is no precise documentation concerning Gilles' criminal activities in France. We do not know, for example, how many children may have died during the many months Gilles spent in Orléans.

Gilles did not procure the children himself. For that he relied, initially, on his cousins Gilles de Sillé and Robert de Briqueville. We do not know how he approached them, or how he articulated his demands. Perhaps by the time of his trial his crimes had become such a matter of routine that no one could recall the first tentative steps. Not that either de Sillé or de Briqueville would have demurred. For his own part, Gilles was concerned at first that knowledge of his activities should be restricted to as few people as possible. He was to be less discreet later.

The first documented case is that of a boy called Jeudon, who had been apprenticed to a local furrier, Guillaume Hilairet. He was about twelve years old. One day Gilles de Sillé, accompanied by Robert de Briqueville, asked Hilairet 'to lend him the said servant to go and take a message to the castle of Machecoul, and the said Hilairet lent him and sent him to the said castle'. Later that same day, when the boy did not return, Hilairet asked de Sillé and de Briqueville where he was. They replied 'that they did not know, unless he had gone to Tiffauges and in such a place, said the aforementioned Sillé, thieves had carried him off to make a page of him'. The boy was never seen again.

It is possible to reconstruct, from the evidence given at the trial, what the boy's fate must have been. He was pampered and dressed in better clothes than he had ever known. The evening began with a large meal and heavy drinking, particularly of hippocras which acted as a stimulant. The boy was then taken to an upper room to which only Gilles and his immediate circle were admitted. There he was confronted with the true nature of his situation. The shock thus produced on the boy was probably an initial source of pleasure for Gilles. In his confession Poitou gave the following description of what normally then took place:

He declared that the said Gilles de Rais, in order to practise his libidinous pleasure and unnatural vices on the said children, both boys and girls, first took his member in his hand and stroked it until it was erect, then placed it between the thighs of the said girls, rubbing his member on the bellies of the said boys and girls with great delight, vigour and libidinous pleasure until the sperm was ejaculated on their bellies.

He declared that before perpetrating his debauches on the

said boys and girls, to prevent them from crying out, and so that they should not be heard, the said Gilles de Rais sometimes hung them up by the neck with ropes, with his own hand, from a hook. Then he would take them down and pretend to comfort them, assuring them that he wished them no harm, but quite the reverse; that he wanted to play with them, and in this manner he prevented them from crying out.

He declared that when the said Gilles de Rais, the accused, committed his horrible debauches and sins of luxury he afterwards killed them or had them killed.

Asked by whom, he replied that sometimes the accused Gilles killed them with his own hand, sometimes he had them killed by the said Sillé, or by Henriet,* or by the witness himself. . . .

Asked in what manner, he replied sometimes by decapitating them, sometimes by cutting their throats, sometimes by dismembering them, sometimes by breaking their necks with a stick, and that there was a weapon specially for their execution, known in the vernacular as a *braquemard*†.

Asked whether the said Gilles de Rais committed his vices on the said children, boys and girls, once only or more times, he answered once only, or twice at most, with each of them.

He further testified that the said Gilles de Rais sometimes committed his vices on the said boys and girls before wounding them, but rarely; other times, and that often, it was after hanging them up or before other wounds; other times it was after he had cut, or caused to be cut, the vein in the neck or the throat so that the blood gushed out; and other times it was as they were dying; other times it was after they were dead and their heads had been cut off, while there remained some warmth in their body.

He testified that the said Gilles de Rais practised his luxurious vices in the same way on girls and boys, disdaining their sexual organs, and he heard him say that he took infinitely more pleasure in debauching himself in this manner

* Henriet Griart and Poitou were Gilles' two bodyservants.
† Quoted in French in the Latin text. A braquemard was a short, thick, double-edged sword.

with the said girls, as has been said above, than in using their natural orifice, in the normal manner.

Gilles added the following details in his own confession :

When the said children were dead he kissed them and those who had the most handsome limbs and heads he held up to admire them, and had their bodies cruelly cut open and took delight at the sight of their inner organs; and very often when the said children were dying he sat on their stomachs and took pleasure in seeing them die and laughed. . . .

This was confirmed by Henriet in his confession :

He testified that he had heard the accused Gilles say that he took more pleasure in the murder of the said children, and in seeing their heads and limbs separated from their body, in seeing them die and their blood flow, than in having carnal knowledge of them.

He stated that the accused, Gilles, . . . often took delight in gazing at the heads that had been cut off, and showed them to the witness and to . . . Etienne Corillaut [Poitou] . . . asking them which of the heads he showed them was the most beautiful, the one which had just been cut off or the one from the night before or the one from the night before that, and that he often kissed the head he liked most, and it gave him much pleasure.

When Poitou was asked what became of the bodies he answered

. . . that they burned them and their clothes. Asked who put them in the fire, he answered that he himself and the said Henriet did it, often.

Asked as to the place where they were burned, he answered in the room of the said Gilles. . . .

Asked in what manner, he answered in the fireplace in the room of the said Gilles, with great logs of wood, by placing faggots on the dead bodies and then lighting a huge fire. The clothes were placed one by one on the fire and held in it, so that they burned more slowly and did not make such a bad smell.

Questioned as to the place where the ashes were thrown, he answered sometimes into the cesspit, other times in the moats or other hiding places. . . .

This was the normal pattern which was followed in almost every case over the next seven years, wherever Gilles happened to be in residence.

Soon children were being regularly supplied to him not only by de Sillé and de Briqueville but also by an old woman, Perrine Martin, who came to be known as 'La Meffraye' (The Terror) among the local populace. She roamed the countryside, enticing any children she came across wandering or tending animals. Gradually the circle of those involved widened, either by accident or design.

It was some time near the beginning of 1437, for example, that Poitou was let into his master's secrets, ten years after he had entered Gilles' service. In 1440 Poitou gave two conflicting accounts of his relationship with Gilles: The first was at the ecclesiastical trial where he stated

> that the said accused Gilles performed the said carnal act on him on one occasion in the manner already described, and that as soon as the said witness came to live with the said Gilles [i.e. 1427], and that he was afraid he might be killed by him; and he thinks he might well have been, and that with a dagger, had not the said de Sillé prevented the said Gilles from doing so, saying that he was a handsome lad and it would be better if Gilles kept him as a page; and the said accused took a liking to him, the witness, and made him swear that he would in no wise reveal any of his secrets.

However, subsequently, at the civil trial, he stated

> that about ten years after he came to live with the said Sire de Rais, whose page he had been for five years, and during the period in which Messire Robert de Briqueville had charge of his affairs, and that after five other years in which he had become a servant of the bedchamber of the said lord, in a period of some two or three months he saw two dead children in the bedchamber of the said lord, who would have killed him but was prevented from so doing by Messires Robert and de Sillé; that afterwards he was kept locked in a room for four days by the said Messire Robert, and, this done, they made him swear to reveal nothing of what he had seen or of what he would see later, but before the oath the said lord had relations with the said Corillaut on the belly.

Both accounts may well refer to real incidents, a decade apart, with elements so similar as to lead Poitou to confuse them. He may well have been seduced as a boy and saved, and have stumbled on his master's secrets and been saved again. Gilles, his mind befuddled by excessive drinking and innumerable crimes, may have forgotten that he once had relations with Poitou as a boy and may have taken him again as a kind of act of initiation. The kind of protection Poitou received from both de Sillé and de Briqueville may be indicative of their own sexual proclivities. Why should they bother to save this particular boy? It is difficult not to conclude that whatever profit they may have derived from their master's deviations those in Gilles' immediate circle were bound together by a certain vicious complicity.

Immediately after this second incident Poitou was admitted fully to the conspiracy:

> Item, he stated that Messire Robert and de Sillé commanded him to lay his hands on children and bring them to the said lord.

Of all the people involved in a history of crime almost without redeeming elements, Poitou is perhaps the most tragic; corrupted and perverted as a child, he was drawn willy-nilly into a situation from which, for him, there was no escape. And from being a passive bystander he was slowly turned into an active participant.

Henriet Griart was the next to be initiated. He was sent to Nantes to collect the brother of Catherine Thierry, wife of a painter. The child was ostensibly being brought to Machecoul to become a member of the chapel. Henriet accepted the story at its face value, brought the child to Machecoul and delivered him to Gilles' room. There Gilles then

> made the witness swear that he would reveal none of the secrets that would be entrusted to him. Questioned on the place where the said oath was given he answered in the church of the Holy Trinity at Machecoul.
>
> Questioned as to the date he said about three years previously. He further added that after he, the witness, had delivered the said child he went to Nantes where he stayed for

three days without returning to Machecoul; and when, returning to Machecoul after three days, he looked for the said child and could not find him, he was told that he (the child) had left this world in the same way as the others, and the said Corillaut, otherwise known as Poitou, informed him that the said accused, Gilles, had killed the said child by his own hand, and that, just like the others, it had served his libidinous acts.

Henriet was apparently trapped into complicity. Perhaps Gilles and his henchmen had decided that since one body servant was party to the secret it would be safer to implicate the second. Having been involved in the procuring of a child, he was made to swear an oath not to reveal a secret which was only confided to him afterwards. Once trapped in this way he actively selected children from among those who came to the castle gate to beg alms.

Machecoul was a small community and it was not long before parents who had lost children began to talk and compare their experiences. They could not possibly guess what had really become of their children; they were not even sure that they were dead. The rumour began to spread, according to Jeanne Edelin, 'that these children had been taken to give to the English to free Messire Michel de Sillé, who was a prisoner of the English, or so people said. And the men of the supposed gentlemen were supposed to have said that they were obliged to supply twenty-four male children to the English as ransom for the said Michel.'
Michel de Sillé's capture at Lagny provided a convenient excuse and would explain his brother's activity in enticing children away. The enemy, pictured in simple minds as being synonymous with the powers of darkness, were believed to be capable of any cruelty, including demanding innocent children whom they wanted, according to Macé Sorin, as pages.
Parents learned to bear their grief in silence, or if they did venture to protest they were quickly silenced. The mother of Guillaume Delit, murdered one February or March, eventually went to the Hotel de la Suze looking for her son some time in May. There she told Madame Briand, wife of one of the men in Gilles' service, 'that it was rumoured that the Sire de Rais had small children taken so that he could kill them'. At that

moment two of Gilles' men arrived and Madame Briand reported her words immediately, stating 'that she would pay dearly for them, and so would others'. Madame Delit then 'begged the pardon of the servants of the said lord' and left.

What is remarkable here is the delay of almost two months before the mother made enquiries. She had received an oblique warning from Jean Briand some time during Lent. He told her that he had seen the boy helping Gilles' cook, Cherpy, to prepare the roast. He added that he had told the cook it was a mistake to let the boy work there. Mme Delit had heard the rumours. Presumably she only spoke to Mme Briand because of the information the woman's husband had given her, and she thought she could trust her. None the less there was a considerable delay.

This story illustrates the cruel dilemma in which parents found themselves. Most of them lived in extreme poverty, with a daily struggle for food and warmth. A child, at its worst, was a mouth to feed. For most there was no escape from their circumstances. If a child was bright, he could be educated by the Church and become a priest or enter a monastery. If not, his one hope of escaping the eternal struggle for survival was to enter the service of a great noble, or be noticed by him and win his favour. As a last resort he could be sent out to beg. Time and time again, in reading the evidence of bereaved parents, one is struck by the ambiguity of their statements, by the conflict in their minds. They knew, or many of them, certainly, the rumours which were current, yet they still sent their children to beg at the castle gates or allowed them to go 'into service' as pages. Mme Delit may well have been relieved to know that her son was being fed in Gilles' kitchen and kept in the warm. When he did not return she may have concluded that he was lucky enough to be sleeping there. These considerations may more than have sufficed to obscure her fears, and lead her to disregard Jean Briand's warning. Other parents may have imagined, as people so often do, that it would not happen to *their* child. Desperation may have driven them to take the risk. Occasionally they sent children in pairs, imagining they would be safer. They were not to know that, according to Henriet, 'when the accused Gilles met two boys or girls, brothers or sisters, or other children who lived together, if one of them was to his taste and he did not wish to have carnal knowledge of the other, he had them both brought to him; he only had vicious relations with one of them, but so that the other should not pine for the first he had both their throats cut'.

Gilles' henchmen were precisely aware of the kind of inducements parents would accept; for the most part they played on their ambitions for their children; sometimes they exploited their greed. When Gilles' herald of arms, Pierre Jacquet, known as Princé, enticed a fourteen-year-old boy named Jean Hubert away, both he and his accomplice, a Scots officer called Spadine (or Spalding, as Georges Bataille suggests), made lavish promises concerning the boy's future. When the parents tried to take the boy out of Princé's service, further promises were made. On the last occasion when young Jean Hubert went to see his mother he told her 'that the lord (Gilles) liked him well, and that he had just cleaned his room and that his master (Princé) had given him a big round loaf of bread that had been baked for the said lord, and which he had brought his mother'. The boy's parents must have been well satisfied. After his disappearance, when his father made enquiries Princé continued the fiction saying that 'peradventure the boy was with some upstanding gentleman who would see that he got on'. A loaf of bread and a few vague promises were sufficient to overcome a parent's fears. Any possibility of escape from degradation and poverty had to be seized on.

This was certainly the case with Peronne Loessart. She also had the rare distinction of being one of the few parents to come into direct contact with Gilles himself. She lived in La Roche-Bernard, opposite the inn owned by Jean Colin where Gilles happened to be staying. She had a boy of ten who was attending school. It was not long before Poitou spotted him and approached his mother. He made the usual promises; 'he said he would dress the boy well and see that he had every advantage.' Peronne replied that she preferred the boy to remain at school. Poitou agreed to continue the boy's education. He then offered an inducement to Peronne herself: 'he would give this Peronne 100 *sous* for a dress'. This was conclusive, for, by her own admission, 'trusting in this promise, she allowed him to take the boy away with him'.

She was not short of attempting a little trickery herself and tried to get a little more money out of the transaction. When Poitou brought her the 100 *sous* 'she remarked that there were 20 *sous* short: he denied this, saying that he had only promised her 4 *livres* [100 *sous*]. She then told him that she concluded it would be difficult for him to keep his other promises as 20 *sous* were missing already. At which he told her not to make a fuss and he would give other gifts, both to her and the child. He then took the child away to the house of Jean Colin.'

Peronne still did not give up. The next day, probably anxious to do the best she could for her child, she waited outside the inn until Gilles came out. She then recommended her son to him. Gilles did not reply; he did not even look at her, but turned to Poitou and said 'that the boy had been well chosen and that he was as pretty as an angel'. Peronne could have had no idea of the significance of these remarks. Her highest hopes must have been confirmed when Poitou bought the boy a horse the next day from the landlord. Two months later he saw it in Nantes being ridden by someone else.

It was cruelly easy to trap deprived and ignorant people into parting with their children. They had no hope of redress. The rights of a great feudal baron like Gilles were almost absolute. Parents could only wait until someone in authority took up their cause. Alas, the time would not be politically right for some years to come.

9

The Prodigal

If Gilles' sexual crimes were pushed to the limits of the imagination so was the extravagance of his daily life. He set about creating a private world only surpassed in splendour by the Roman emperors he had been so fond of reading about when a boy. Life in most castles was lavish but Gilles felt somehow compelled to outshine them all. His castles at Champtocé and Tiffauges looked like fortresses, dark and forbidding, but inside they had been transformed. He filled them with fine furniture, pictures, statues, gold and silver work, books and precious manuscripts. The chapel in the Hôtel de la Suze, which his grandfather had built at Nantes, was given a painted ceiling and stained-glass windows of the highest quality, while other rooms were hung with cloth of gold, for which he paid from sixty to eighty *écus* a yard. Neither the Duke of Brittany nor any of his household could compete on those terms.

Gilles kept a personal army of 200 to 250 men, whom he equipped with the finest horses, and whom he supplied with complete new liveries three times a year. He had jugglers, singers and actors in his service, and innumerable servants to supply their needs.

Wherever he went—and like his royal master he tended to move from residence to residence—he kept open house to anyone and everyone, nobles and commoners alike. People who lived in the district, or who were merely passing through, could stop at the castle and find food and drink. The tables were always laid. Sometimes Gilles would give away entire liveries, consisting of over a hundred separate garments, to total strangers, people who had no connection with his household or his affairs. The *Mémoire des Héritiers* records that on at least one occasion he pushed generosity so far that there was nothing left for him 'when he wished to dine or sup because there was neither provision nor husbandry'. Such prodigious spending had never been seen before, nor was it seen after, and his reputation spread throughout the countryside, at Champtocé, Machecoul, Tiffauges, Nantes and Orléans.

During the period he spent at Machecoul—most of 1433 and 1434—Gilles embarked upon a project which he valued more than anything else in life, the foundation of his own chapel, the Chapel of the Holy Innocents. It is impossible to say whether he was conscious of the black irony implicit in his choice of title, but just as he admired the severed heads of his victims, so he admired his 'little angels' who both looked and sounded as though they had come straight from heaven. In founding his own *'Collégiale'* he could satisfy his passion for beautiful children and for music as well. Both church music and ceremonial had reached intoxicating and elaborate heights. The theatre of the world where he had played a leading part with Joan was replaced by the theatre of his own establishment, which only needed a religious foundation to complete it.

As with everything else, the chapel was organised on a scale unparalleled anywhere else. He poured money into it. According to the *Mémoire des Héritiers,* no one could 'remember or believe that they had ever seen such superfluity, such excess, such unreasonable expenditure in the chapel of a prince or a king of France'.

The establishment proper consisted of about thirty people:

... children, chaplains, young clerks and others; he took them with him on his travels in such manner that he had in his train . . . including their servants, more than fifty people, at his expense, and as many horses. Likewise, he had in this chapel a quantity of ornaments, cloth of gold, silk, candlesticks, censers, crosses, plate of great luxury.... Likewise in this said chapel, there was a dean, choirboys, archdeacons, curates, a school-master ... as in a cathedral ... some he paid 4 *écus*, others 300, as well as all their expenses.

Their costumes, which he designed himself, were equally lavish: 'he dressed them in trailing robes of scarlet with best quality furs, with squirrel . . . and other fine plumes and furs. . . .' The choir wore 'surplices of the finest cloth, bonnets and hats made and lined with squirrel-fur, as though they had been of great consequence and learning ... such as the canons of cathedral churches are accustomed to wear'. Special clothes were designed for travel: 'He had hooded capes and robes of the finest cloth made for them, but short, so that they might ride more conveniently.'

Gilles had a goldsmith in his service to provide the church plate:

> The portable candlesticks and those for the altar, the censers, the crosses and chalices, the ciboria, the reliquaries, among which was the silver head of Saint-Honoré, were made of solid gold and silver, adorned with precious stones, finely engraved, set with brilliant enamels, and the perfection of the craftsmanship surpassed the richness of the material.

He also had several organs constructed, some big, some small, and even portable organs, which needed six men to carry them, so that he should not be deprived of music when he was obliged to travel.

Gilles' family were quite right in stating that the foundation was worthy of a cathedral, for Gilles, entirely on his own initiative, and without consulting the church authorities, created the dean of the chapel bishop. The Pope, who had received a protest from his outraged relatives, refused to recognise the appointment but this did not deter Gilles. The head of the chapel of the Holy Innocents always received the title and style of a bishop.

Gilles brought the same concern to the quality of the singing in the chapel as he had to the plate and vestments. He wanted the finest boys' voices and he was prepared to pay for them. Two names have come down to us; the first is André Buchet and the other is Rossignol, a boy who was so called because of his voice. Gilles heard him sing one day in Poitiers and immediately wanted him for his chapel. He paid his parents 300 *écus* in cash and settled the property of La Rivière, near Machecoul, with an annual income of 200 *livres* on the boy. He had him brought to Machecoul in great style, 'as though he were a boy of some consequence or from a great family.' Within a short space of time both André Buchet and Rossignol were corrupted by Gilles, sexually, and later played a more active rôle in his crimes. It seems that when Gilles did not feel a homicidal urge he contented himself by having relations with his choir-boys, one of whom, Perrinet, was known as his 'little darling'.

Gilles completed his household with a typically theatrical gesture. He created a facsimile of himself. He took one of his servants, named him 'Rais le Héraut', dressed him magnificently and used him as a substitute. 'Rais le Héraut' had a place of honour in the cortège when Gilles and his household rode out, and was prominent on all public occasions. He offered Gilles a mirror of himself, so that he could be both actor and spectator at once.

*   *   *   *

In March 1434 Gilles was obliged to leave his private pursuits and fulfil his duties as Marshal of France. He had not been entirely alienated from the court after La Trémoille's fall. His money and troops were still useful. The king summoned him to Sillé-le-Guillaume where Arthur de Richemont planned to do battle with the English. The other commanders were very obviously of de Richemont's faction; Charles d'Anjou, Yolande d'Aragon's son, was titular leader of the army; Jean de Bueil was present, as were d'Alençon and Gilles' cousin Guy de Laval-Lohéac. In the event the whole enterprise was a waste of time and money. The two armies lined up, looked at each other and rode away in opposite directions. The most impressive feature of the occasion was the resplendent turn-out of Gilles' men.

Gilles was about to ride back to his estates when La Trémoille called on him for help. Like his rival Arthur de Richemont, Georges de la Trémoille was tenacious in defeat and equally determined to make himself useful and show how indispensable he was. He still had hopes of winning back the king's favour.

The town of Grancey, where La Trémoille still had some influence, was under siege by the Duke of Burgundy's troops. La Trémoille had two companies of his own troops in the area and he suggested to Gilles that if they combined forces they might raise the siege. For the first time Gilles replied that he had no money. La Trémoille offered to lend him 10,000 *réaux*, on the assurance that the king would reimburse him but taking Champtocé as security for safe measure. Charles agreed to the expedition, so there seemed little risk of anyone making a loss financially. But Gilles was no longer interested. He had been called on once to no purpose and forced to abandon what were now to him more pressing concerns. He took the loan and sent his brother René in his place. Then, much to Charles VII's annoyance, he rode back to Poitiers.

René de la Suze was not so good a soldier as his brother. He lacked flair, the sheer insanity of Gilles' risk-taking. The campaign was a failure and Grancey surrendered to Philippe le Bon on 15 August 1434. On the same day Gilles had the foundation of his chapel made official and had himself created Canon of Saint-Hilaire de Poitiers, probably for no other reason except that he wished to wear the ecclesiastical robes which he had designed himself. He was also the first person to bear this title since the dukes of Aquitaine, and this doubtless appealed to his sense of the magnificent. On the same day he also created two livings for his favourite singers, André Buchet and Rossignol.

Gilles' deliberate abandonment of his military duties in favour of his own private pursuits marks a significant turning-point in his career. Hitherto he had always found great stimulus on the battlefield. He enjoyed slaughter and the sight of blood. But now this need was satisfied elsewhere. Public life had become tedious. It was an unrewarding game. He had known the heroic days of Orléans and the lightning campaign along the Loire valley. He had been honoured at Reims. Now all that could be offered to him was the frustrating stand-off at Sillé-le-Guillaume.

From Poitiers Gilles moved to Orléans where his brother René de la Suze and his cousin Guy de Laval-Lohéac joined him. This is the only occasion in the whole of their adult lives that the two brothers are recorded as having been together. His journey from Poitiers must have resembled a royal progress. At the head of the procession rode his living effigy, Rais le Héraut, then came Gilles himself with his cousins Gilles de Sillé and Robert de Briqueville. After them came some 250 men-at-arms, followed by the members of the chapel and their servants. Innumerable pack-horses carried personal possessions, church plate and vestments, not forgetting the portable organs. In all some 400 people must have been involved.

Orléans was a logical choice for Gilles to make. He had known his moments of greatest glory there; the townsfolk honoured him as a hero. The change in political climate had not altered that. Moreover when he arrived money arrived with him, and the local inn-keepers and tradesmen could be sure of being in pocket. Indeed, that September Gilles and his men occupied every inn, tavern and lodging house in the town. The list gives us some idea of the extent of Gilles' household. He himself lodged at the 'Croix-d'Or', which was probably a private house, and his brother at the 'Petit Saumon'. The chapel lodged at the 'Ecu de Saint-Georges', the dean at the 'Enseigne de l'Epée' and his men-at-arms and the herald at the 'Tête Noire'. His Captain of the Guard, Louis l'Angevin, Gilles de Sillé, Guy de Bannière, Guyot de Chambrays, Guillaume Tardif, and Guy de Blanchefort were at the 'Grand Saumon'. His knights, de Martigné Foulques Blasmes, Jean de Rains and Bauléis, went to the 'Image de Sainte Marie-Madeleine'. Jean de Montecler lodged with Colin le Godelier; Hector Broisset, his personal armourer, at the 'Coupe'. Gilles' horse, along with those of his brother, were cared for at the 'Roche-Boulet'; the horses belonging to the chapel, Ollinet, Petit-Jean, Le Blond, a priest and his barber went to the 'Enseigne du Fourbisseur'. Jean de Vierille, a nobleman, Boisoulier, Gilles' provost, Georges, a trumpeter, and Thomas, who illuminated Gilles' books, went to the 'Dieu d'Amour'. The remaining servants were divided among the 'Cheval Blanc', the 'Homme Sauvage' and the 'Ecu d'Orléans'.* And, in the words of the *Mémoire des Héritiers*, 'those who had the management of his household lived in their lodgings at great and excessive expense, and like great lords, and all at the cost of the said ... Sire de Rais'.

Unfortunately Gilles did not have the money to meet these expenses. Nor, as it turned out, was he able to finance his next project, the production of a mystery play in which one of the parts was a portrayal of himself at his moment of greatest glory.

---

* The original of this list of lodgings was lost in a fire in Orléans in 1940, but was fortunately reproduced in the Abbé Bossard's book.

10

Le Mistère du Siège a'Orléans

Gilles' principal reason for going to Orléans was to mount this production. 'Le Mistère du Siège d'Orléans' was to be presented on 8 May 1435, the tenth anniversary of the raising of the siege. The play is a huge one, running to some 20,000 lines of verse.* It contains 140 speaking parts and calls for anything up to 500 extras. There were costumes to be made and scenery to be built. The play moves from place to place with the rapidity of a film. The cost of staging would be enormous, and while the municipal authorities defrayed some of the expenses the main burden fell on Gilles' willing shoulders. Unfortunately, Gilles was almost bankrupt. Those shopkeepers and tradespeople who had rubbed their hands at his arrival were due to have their credit sorely stretched.

It seems inconceivable that he should have been short of money. His lands were estimated to be worth 30,000 *livres*; the pensions and salaries which he received as Marshal of France raised this to about 50,000 *livres,* and he owned books, furniture and objets d'art to the value of 100,000 *écus.*† No one in France, or for that matter in Europe, possessed such a fortune.

Yet he had already been short of money when he sold Blaison in 1429. Since then he had poured out rivers of money to finance his pleasures. Nothing could stop him; whatever he wanted he must have. Matters were not helped by the fact that he was systematically cheated. He paid two or three times the real price for almost everything he purchased, from the commonest household wares to the most precious and costly materials —sixty *écus* a yard for cloth of gold worth thirty at the most; and it was a material he used lavishly. The constant cry of his outraged relatives in the *Mémoire des Héritiers* is that he bought

* The text we now possess runs to some 25,000 lines but this is the result of later additions.

† Roughly £1,250,000 sterling in current values.

dear and sold cheap. There is every reason to suppose, moreover, that his cousins, Gilles de Sillé and Robert de Briqueville, lined their own pockets at his expense, taking a liberal commission on every transaction.

The fact is that he could not afford any of the elaborate schemes he embarked on after his grandfather's death. He began selling property as early as April 1432. On the 8th he sold Fontaine-Milon to Jean de Marseilles for a mere 4,000 *écus*, which was well below its real value. The sales continued regularly.

At first only lands on the periphery of the Rais estates were disposed of, perhaps in an attempt to soften the blow. Familiar names appear among the list of purchasers. Guillaume de la Jumellière, who had been Gilles' mentor and guide during his first campaigns, acquired Blaison and Chamelier for 5,000 *écus*, although he in fact paid only 3,000. Hardouin de Bueil, who had officiated at Gilles' wedding, bought Chemié and Grattecuisse for 5,000 *écus*. Jean de Pontclerc, who was in Gilles' service, acquired Sénéché and Voulte-en-Poitou for 6,000 *écus*; Jean de Malestroit, Bishop of Nantes, and no friend of Gilles' bought Brégny for 14,000 *écus*. In fact he did not part with any cash but merely wrote a promissory note. La Mothe-Achard went to Guy de la Roche-Guyon, who had once been Gilles' rival for the hand of Jeanne Paynal.

Other properties were acquired, nominally, at least, by tradesmen and merchants in Angers, some of whom were already lending Gilles money at 10 per cent. The names of Perrinet Pain, Guillaume le Cesne, Guillaume Trémière, Pierre Bérard, and du Chabot have come down to us. These men were sufficiently aware of Gilles' difficulties, moreover, to make him accept part of any loan in kind—silks, cloth of gold, tapestries—which Robert de Briqueville then had to re-sell, usually at far less than their real value, and at a profit to himself. Indeed so many people were engaged in sharp practice that Gilles had no hope of receiving the full value of his property.

By March 1433 he had sold off all his estates in Poitou except those belonging to his wife; he had nothing left in Maine, and only two castles, Champtocé and Ingrandes, in Anjou. The total sales and mortgages brought him in 180–200,000 *écus* (i.e.

between £1,750,000 and £2,000,000 sterling at current rates). At least half was spent on the production of the play.

Gilles' original intention was doubtless to stay in Orléans from the autumn of 1434 until the following summer, preparing this great spectacle, but La Trémoille, who was still trying to win back the king's favour, made a sudden call on his services with a plan to go to the aid of the Duc de Bourbon in his pursuit of the war. He arrived in Orléans and was able to force his young cousin to help him. They left Orléans together, surrounded by an enormous retinue.

In October Gilles was in Montluçon where he ran up a bill of 800 *réaux* at the 'Ecu de France'. He was not able to pay more than 195 *réaux* and consequently left two servants behind as security before moving on. What became of the expedition is unknown, but it could not have been very successful for by December Gilles was back once more in Orléans, where on the 28th he signed a document giving Robert de Briqueville complete power of attorney to transact all business relating to the sale of his estates. De Briqueville was given authority to dispose of all property in Brittany, the one remaining region where Gilles had anything left, and he was empowered to arrange a marriage for Marie de Rais, Gilles' daughter, who was barely four years old, and to fix the dowry at any sum he chose. It was a most extraordinary document for anyone to sign and indicates how obsessed Gilles was becoming with the problem of ready money. He no longer cared where it came from so long as it was to hand when he needed it.

He stayed in Orléans until February 1435 when La Trémoille arrived with another scheme for a campaign. Gilles was even less enthusiastic than he had been on the last occasion, but his treaty with his cousin was still valid and he had received many favours in the past. La Trémoille's idea was to engage the Duke of Burgundy's forces, but while they were travelling towards such scattered fighting as there was Charles and Philippe le Bon signed a treaty, on February 5, at Arras and the fighting stopped. La Trémoille refused to give up. Jean de Luxembourg, one of Philippe's allies, refused to recognise the treaty and laid siege to the town of Laon. La Tremoille decided to ride north and raise the siege. But money was short and the days when Gilles paid his troops without question were over. It was agreed, therefore, that he should go to Lyon and try to raise money. This he did, but on his return the amount proved too small and the troops refused to fight. It was evident that Gilles had been cheated by the financiers as usual. La Trémoille was frankly amused. Gilles then suggested that he should return to Orléans and try to raise money there. Perhaps La Trémoille believed him, or perhaps he realised that it was just an excuse for Gilles to return to more agreeable pursuits. At all events he agreed, but not before he made Gilles sign a document, at Langres, bequeathing Champtocé to him should he and his brother René die without heirs. This doubtless was to indemnify him for the 12,000 *réaux* he had lent the year before, although he was already entitled to 1,200 *réaux* per annum from the estate as repayment.

By the end of February Gilles was back in Orléans trying to raise money. He sold or pawned the silver head of Saint-Honoré, his most precious relic. Having sold off most of his lands, he was reduced to getting rid of personal possessions. However, he had no intention of wasting the money on a campaign of doubtful issue. The bulk of what he had left was intended for the production of the play and the maintenance of his chapel, which he intended to secure for all time. He had two lawyers, Jean Caseau and Jean de Réconin, draw up a document confirming the foundation of the Chapel of the Holy Innocents in perpetuity, which he signed on March 26.

It is an elaborate and in many ways insanely worded statement, illustrating Gilles' obsession with his chapel and his fear of what his relatives might do after his death. Signs of disapproval from his family must have been already reaching him. His brother René and his cousin Guy were with him in Orléans and could see the rate at which money was being spent. As for the mass sale of property, this must have been a matter of public scandal, and his relatives must have been outraged to see the conventions of their class so wildly flouted. The document reveals how much Gilles was aware of this and the irrational nature of his reaction. First the foundation made at Machecoul is confirmed, then he states that, should his wife and daughter refuse to carry out his wishes, he will leave Champtocé to René d'Anjou and other lands to the Duke of Brittany, so that they can maintain them. (He seems to have forgotten that he had just bequeathed Champtocé to La Trémoille.) Should they refuse, he will leave the property to the king; should the king refuse it will go to the Emperor, and so on through the Pope, finally ending with the Order of Saint John of Jerusalem.

His wishes could not possibly have been carried out under any circumstances, but Gilles seems to have believed in the magical power of this paper to conjure his wishes into being.

*   *   *   *

Preparations for the play were now going forward. Gilles ordered that all costumes for the play, over 600 of them, were to be made from new material. Even rags were to be created by slashing fine cloth. He further ordered that the same costume was not to be worn twice, so that there would be a fresh set for every performance, if more than one took place.

Debts were piling up and a certain number of payments had to be made. On April 16 he pawned 'a cope, a scarlet mantle, figured in green, woven with small golden birds, adorned with a hood and worked with gold, together with a chasuble and a deacon's dalmatic.' For these he received 64 *réaux* and 14 *sous* from Jean de Laon, a furrier.

On the 30th he pawned 'two hoods for a church cope, one embroidered with the Trinity, the other with the coronation of Our Lady; a cope of crushed velvet with cloth of gold, worked with gold with images in pairs; a dalmatic of figured satin, black, with silk; a Cyprus canopy thirteen yards in length, woven with gold'. These items came from his own chapel and give a further idea of the luxury with which he surrounded himself. It is impossible to say what fraction of the original cost the money he received represented.

At all events, creditors were somehow satisfied and the 'Mistère du Siège d'Orléans' duly received its first performance on 8 May 1435. An elaborate stage had been constructed, with multiple décor, and large enough to enable several hundred actors to reconstruct the events of the siege, and to give a convincing impression of movement from place to place. Gilles also arranged that unlimited supplies of food and drink should be available to all the spectators, so that several thousand people were entertained and fed at his expense that day.

In the four years since Joan's execution legend had already taken over from history, and the picture of events presented by the play was a highly idealised one. Joan is a saint and Gilles is her faithful servant. The early squabbles, the initial mistrust, are glossed over. Gilles wanted a glamorised picture of himself held up for public admiration—that was why he had financed the performance. It has been suggested that he took part himself as an actor, but there is no evidence for this and it seems unlikely. He would have enjoyed watching himself much more, and it is possible that there were three Gilles de Rais on view that day, Gilles himself, Rais le Héraut, and the actor on the stage.

Gilles watched his own appointment as commander in chief of the army:

Charles:
And to lead, your men
Shall have the Marshal de Rais,
A valiant gentleman.
Ambroise de Loré also;
To both I give express command
To lead you where you will.
Gilles:
Lady, what is your will to do?

The deliberate deception practised on Joan as to the route to be taken to Orléans is not mentioned. Perhaps the author knew nothing of it.

The picture of Gilles as a model and faithful companion is everywhere reinforced.

Gilles:
Lady, if it is your will to depart
Here are your men in all things ready.

Later he assures Joan of his full support:

Lady, have no doubt of me
I wish but to do your will.
My friends and underlings,
Know, lady, all shall come
And we shall do your will.
In everything.

In the scene representing the storming of Les Tourelles, the psychological climax of the Orléans campaign, Gilles' own banner was used to add a touch of authenticity.

We see him later in a council of war, at which Joan is not present, urging her view that no more time should be wasted in campaigning but that they should push on to Reims for the coronation:

> We should refuse her nothing,
> And have no doubt of victory
> Since she is at the head.

Although Gilles has fine moments in the play, in terms of length his rôle is by no means a leading one, considerably less than that of Dunois, but he was evidently satisfied with the showing he was given. He may even have financed other, shorter plays during the festivities.

The mortgaging went on to finance this extravagance. On May 20 de Briqueville mortgaged 300 *livres* from the income of Bourgneuf for 6,000 *livres* in cash and began negotiations for the sale of La Mothe-Achard, Chénies and Manières to the Duke of Brittany for the sum of 21,500 *écus*. On June 7 Gilles pawned the gold candlesticks from his chapel and on the 14th he was obliged to leave his favourite horse, Casse-Noisette, together with his saddle and harness, another black horse and eight others in settlement of the debts he and his two personal servants had incurred. On the 20th he bought arms from Colon Mauneveu on credit.

By this time René de la Suze had seen more than enough. His own direct inheritance had been assured the previous year when on January 25 Gilles had surrendered the lands due to him under his father's and his grandfather's will: the de la Suze and Briolay estates, income from Loreux-Bottereau, Boing and Champtocé, and the property that had belonged to Jean de Craon near Laon and in the Champagne district. Even so, some of this had been eaten into and no noble family could tolerate the dissipation of its wealth, in which a collective pride was taken, or the loss of reputation that such wild extravagance brought. A few properties still remained, more especially those belonging to Catherine de Rais, Gilles' unfortunate wife.

At some time during June 1435 a meeting was held by the various branches of the family, the Lavals, the Lohéacs, the Châtillons, René de la Suze, Catherine de Rais and possibly even La Trémoille himself. They decided to put a curb on Gilles. They wrote to Pope Eugene IV asking him to disavow the foundation of the Chapel of the Holy Innocents: 'Our Holy Father, being appraised of the actions and the conduct of the late Seigneur de Rais, and being informed that they were due to madness and simpleness of mind, refused to countenance the matter.' They also appealed to the king and on July 2 a royal edict was proclaimed, describing Gilles as a spendthrift and forbidding him to sell off any further property. No subject of Charles VII was allowed to enter into any contract with him and those in command of his castles were forbidden to hand them over, no matter what the circumstances, or what sums of money had changed hands. The *Parlement* of Poitiers was instructed to appoint an executor to administer the Rais estates. The terms of the edict were made public in Orléans, Tours, Angers, Pouzauges, and Champtocé, where Gilles' former tutor Michel de Fontenay was responsible for its publication. We can only guess at the secret pleasure which Charles may have felt at seeing yet another of those who had treated him with disregard, if not open contempt, get their comeuppance.

Gilles' credit immediately fell, and those who had been only too happy to enjoy and exploit his patronage now pressed him for their money before he left the town to return to his estates. On August 25 he borrowed 260 *réaux d'or* from Charles de Halot, landlord of the 'Cheval Blanc', leaving behind a manuscript of Valerius Maximus, a Latin edition of St Augustine's *City of God,* and a French translation of the same work, as well as two copes, one of damask, and a chasuble of black satin. He also left 'a parchment book, called the *Metamorphoses* of Ovid, bound in scarlet leather, ornamented with brass keys and a silver lock, together with a wooden cross, covered with silver gilt on which there was a crucifix of pure silver', to Jeanette Boilève as security for money which he owed her. When Gilles left Orléans in late August or early September the town was littered with the precious objects he had been forced to leave behind. During the year, on and off, that he had stayed there he had spent £1 million.

Family Reactions

It was one thing to issue a royal edict, it was another to enforce
it. No executor was ever appointed by the *Parlement* of Poitiers,
which felt that a tactful silence was the wisest course of action.
Whatever had happened to Gilles in recent years he was still
a dangerous man with considerable power. The edict, moreover,
did not apply to Brittany and all attempts by Gilles' relatives to
persuade Jean V to enforce it failed.

As for Gilles, he let it be known that he would have nothing
more to do with any member of his family, except his brother.
His wife had been living apart from him for some time at
Pouzauges and as far as he was concerned she could stay there.
His last demand on her was made in November 1435 when he
obliged her to sign all the rights to Prinçay and Bourgneuf over
to him. Robert de Briqueville then raised 20,000 *réaux* from
the Duke of Brittany in return for 1,000 *réaux* per annum from
the income. No further contact between Gilles and his wife is
recorded in his lifetime.

Jean V had sound personal reasons for refusing to ratify
Charles' edict. He had noted Gilles' increasing dissipation and
had decided to use it to his own advantage. Gilles' estates cut
right across the frontier between France and Brittany, giving
some of his possessions, Champtocé and Ingrandes in particular,
considerable strategic importance. Even at the time when Jeanne
Chabot was looking for an heir, Jean IV, the present Duke's
father, had tried to get hold of them. Jean V inherited his father's
ambition. By lending Gilles money, he was prepared to lead
him deeper and deeper into debt, so that he could,
later, present an ultimatum. It might take years but he was
willing to pursue a long-term policy. There was only one difficulty from his point of view; the Dukes of Brittany were for-

bidden, by law, to acquire property from their subjects. This he circumvented by using proxies, and it is more than probable that many of the undistinguished merchants who bought estates from Gilles were in fact Jean's agents. At all events he took possession of La Mothe-Achard in Poitou on August 11, although officially it had been sold to Guy de la Roche-Guyon.

Gilles took up residence at Machecoul in the autumn of 1435. It was about this time that Guillaume de la Jumellière left him after being in his service for eight years. La Jumellière seems to have been an honest man. Perhaps he was shocked by the riotous extravagance he saw, perhaps he had heard rumours of the crimes that took place secretly in the upper room. A mediaeval castle was a small closed community where it was difficult to keep secrets. Besides, the local peasantry were already whispering and asking questions, even if they dared not voice their anxieties and fears too loudly. What was an honest man to do under the circumstances? Cut and run before the storm broke and scandal engulfed them all.

Little precise information is available about Gilles' sexual activities in the last quarter of 1435, but Guillaume Hilairet, whose evidence has already been quoted, made the following statement at the trial:

> Item, the said Guillaume Hilairet declared that about five years previously [i.e. 1435] he heard a certain Jean du Jardin, who lodged with Messire Robert de Briqueville, say they had found a pipe full of dead children at Champtocé. Item, this Guillaume Hilairet declared that he heard some time ago a woman on the Rais estates, whose name he does not know, complain that she had lost her child at Machecoul.

This suggests that the murders were taking place regularly.

In May of 1436 Gilles took his revenge on his old tutor Michel de Fontenay for publishing the royal edict against him. Fontenay was a priest at Angers, and had close connections with the University. Passing through the town one day, on an impulse, Gilles broke into Fontenay's home and took him prisoner. He was kept in a dungeon first at Champtocé then at Machecoul. It was a foolish gesture. Gilles and his grandfather had done this sort of thing many times before in the past, but Jean de Craon had always shown better judgment and discretion. He would have thought twice about raising his hand against a cleric who enjoyed the privilege of immunity. However uncertain temporal authority might be, the church still had powerful weapons with which to protect her own. The Bishops of Angers, the University and the municipal authorities all protested, and Gilles was obliged to give way. Fontenay was released. Gilles had gained nothing except the animosity of the clergy, already fairly ill-disposed towards him.

Gilles' family were not prepared to let matters drop. They were aware that Jean V was negotiating the purchase of various properties, whatever subterfuge he might employ; they were aware that his ultimate objective was Champtocé, and they were prepared to block any further move he made to acquire any more of the family's possessions. Jean V, for his part, was conscious of the feeling he had created and suspected a plot against him between René de la Suze and André de Laval-Lohéac. Accordingly, as a precautionary measure, he travelled to Machecoul to obtain individual oaths of allegiance from all the captains in charge of Gilles' domains; from Michel de Sillé, who had finally been ransomed, and his lieutenant Jean de Dresneuc, who were in command at Machecoul; from Conan de Vieilchatel, who commanded Saint-Etienne-de-Mer-Morte; from Yvon de Kersalion, who commanded Pornic; and from Valentin de Moretemer, who commanded Loroux-Bottereau: Jean then summoned both René de la Suze and André de Laval-Lohéac to Nantes, where he obliged them to sign a document affirming their allegiance. They could hardly do otherwise without bringing the dispute out into the open. Besides, André de Laval-Lohéac was Lieutenant-General of Brittany, which placed him in a doubly difficult position.

Gilles' family on their side wanted guarantees about Champtocé, which was now in the centre of everyone's mind. On 13 September 1436, a meeting was held in Ancenis to discuss the whole question. Those present were Charles d'Anjou, first minister of France; Jean V; his brother Arthur de Richemont, René de la Suze, now de Richemont's lieutenant; André de Laval-Lohéac; Dunois; and Gilles' old adversary Jean de Bueil. The purpose of the meeting was to warn off Jean V, to remind him that Champtocé was in France and that reaction would be unfavourable if it passed into Breton hands. Jean V made reassuring noises and the meeting ended with the usual exchange of meaningless letters of alliance and friendship.

Gilles was either unaware of the squabbles going on around him or he chose to ignore them. He had abandoned all interest in the day-to-day running of affairs when he gave Robert de Briqueville such extraordinary and extensive powers, but he did have a sentimental attachment to Champtocé which was his birthplace and he tried to hang on to it as long as he could. Besides, extensive evidence of his crimes had accumulated there, in the cess-pools and the moats where the bones had been jettisoned after the rest of the bodies had been burned.

Gilles' family, in the meantime, were still taking active measures to protect their interests. René d'Anjou, Yolande d'Aragon's eldest son, who had been a prisoner, was released by the Duke of Burgundy and returned to take over control of the government, which had been in the hands of his brother Charles during his absence. Charles had supported the Rais family and they now set about securing René d'Anjou's favour. They asked him to state his firm opposition to the sale of Champtocé and Ingrandes to the Duke of Brittany. They were not slow to remind him that Gilles had attacked his mother two years previously. René d'Anjou's reply was all that they could have wished. He declared that Champtocé was forfeit to him and then demanded that Jean V sign a formal declaration that he had no designs on it. This Jean V did, swearing on 'the body of Our Saviour'. He continued none the less to press Gilles to sell Champtocé and in the meantime on May 26 bought the domain of La Bénate for 10,000 *écus*. He paid Princé, Gilles' herald, sixty *livres* for expediting the affair. The sale was put through in the name of the Duke's son Pierre. In the course of the next few months he gave Guillaume Grimaud and Guillaume Sauzaie, two of Gilles' men, 400 *saluts d'or* apiece, to encourage them to persuade their master to sell Champtocé.

Unfortunately both Gilles and the Duke had overlooked one snag when negotiating the sale of La Bénate. It did not belong to Gilles at all. Jean de Craon had signed it over to his second wife Anne de Sillé, who was still alive and unwilling to be done out of her property. Jean V was therefore unable to take possession. His move, however, was sufficient to alert René le la Suze and André de Laval-Lohéac to the unreliability of his word—though considering past events it is surprising they had any faith in it in the first place—and they decided to settle the matter once and for all. In October 1437 they took Champtocé by force.

Gilles panicked. He felt sure that the occupation of Champtocé was merely a preliminary to the occupation of Machecoul itself. There was incriminating evidence of past crimes at Champtocé, if anyone knew where to look, and there were remains of children's bodies at Machecoul as well. He ordered Gilles de Sillé and another of his men, Robin Romulart (Petit Robin), to dispose of the bones of about forty children 'from a tower near the lower halls of the said castle'. While the work was going on Robert de Briqueville, who for some reason was not involved in the labours, arranged a peep-show for two noble ladies of the district, who were allowed to watch the operations in progress. Gilles de Sillé's comments on this were reported more or less verbatim at the trial: 'Was not Messire Robert de Briqueville a traitor to let Robin Romulart and me be seen by Madame de Jarville and Madame Tremin d'Arraguin, through a crack when we were removing the bones?'

This macabre incident is doubly revealing. On the one hand it indicates how sure Robert de Briqueville felt of his position, however much Gilles might have taken fright. Gilles' reaction was much more prompted by his own feelings of guilt than any genuine, objective danger. The second thing which emerges from this incident is the amused tolerance the two ladies felt towards his aberrations. They felt no horror or disgust at what they saw; they were far more likely to be shocked by his extravagance and the destruction of the family estates. A few peasant children more or less made no difference; they died quickly enough. The feelings of the parents were never considered. They were lower beings who were not supposed to have valid emotions. As part of the cattle on the estate it was not their function to lay claim to a delicate sensibility. The privileges of the aristocracy were inviolable, providing they did not become politically dangerous.

The two ladies were not alone in their attitude which was confirmed when, barely three weeks later, as Gilles had so justly anticipated, René de la Suze and André de Laval-Lohéac occupied Machecoul. Unfortunately de Sillé and Romulart had done a botched job and two skeletons were found. A captain of René de la Suze's troops questioned both Poitou and Henriet on the matter but they denied all knowledge of it. They were lying, of course. Even if they played no direct part in the murders, they knew well enough how they had occurred. The matter was then dropped, and a wall of silence erected round the family. However much they might disapprove of Gilles' behaviour it was no part of their duty to betray him, not on these grounds, at least. Providing the property was safe, whatever else he did was his business. Besides, if they spoke up, the local peasantry might come forward and tell what they knew and the whole family would be plunged into disgrace.

If Gilles was alarmed so was the Duke of Brittany. He could not be certain that the occupation of these two castles would not be followed by a direct attack on his own territory. On November 2 he called a meeting of his vassals at Vannes, to ensure their support. Gilles was present. One cannot help wondering what sort of an appearance he now made, despite his magnificent clothes, after years of heavy drinking and sexual debauchery. But for the moment Jean V still needed him and decided to make a friendly gesture towards a man whom he was secretly trying to ruin. He dismissed André de Laval-Lohéac as Lieutenant-General of Brittany and appointed Gilles in his place, thanking him warmly for his past services. At the same time he sent for his brother, Arthur de Richemont, who had been campaigning against the English. An aggressive posture seemed the best way to discourage an attack.

While Gilles was staying at Vannes, Jean V took the opportunity to urge him to sell Champtocé once and for all. He reminded Gilles that in 1435 he had mortgaged the income from a large part of the Rais estates for a period of three years. The time was nearly up and he would have to find 30,000 *écus*. The Duke then suggested what seemed a generous alternative. If Gilles would cede Champtocé and Ingrande he would receive 100,000 *écus*. Payment was to be made as follows: the Duke would return the estates of Bourgneuf, La Bénate, Prinçé and La Mothe-Achard, worth a total of 53,200 *écus*, and he would also buy back for him the lands he had sold to Jean de Malestroit, the Chapter of Nantes and the Treasurer General, for 46,800 *écus*. As a sop to Gilles' vanity, he gave him the option of buying back the property in six years. It was a perfectly safe offer to make. Gilles would never find the money. Gilles considered the offer and in the meantime on Christmas Day it was his Chapel of Holy Innocents, who always travelled with him, who sang Mass.

Agreement was finally reached on 20 January 1438 immediately after the long Christmas festivities. Jean V acquired the property in the name of his son, Gilles de Bretagne, and it was estimated to be worth 6,000 *livres* a year. The completion of the transaction was of course dependent on Gilles recovering the property from his brother.

René de la Suze's attitude to his brother was ambiguous. He had no great feeling for him, it is true, but he avoided a complete break. Possibly he felt that in the absence of any effective legal sanctions the best method was to salvage what he could from the wreck. He was also aware that, although officially acting in support of the de Rais family, René d'Anjou was planning to place Champtocé under royal control for ever, to prevent any possibility of aggression by Jean V, who might attack an individual nobleman but would hesitate to affront the French court. Under these circumstances Champtocé would still be lost.

Gilles approached his brother and they reached an agreement. In return for Champtocé Gilles offered his brother 7,000 *écus* and the castle of La Mothe-Achard which he would recover under the terms of his agreement with the Duke. In order to save face, a mock assault would be staged and only token resistance offered. In this way René could not be accused of treachery by his royal patrons.

In the early summer, possibly in June, René left Champtocé in the charge of his wife Anne. A mere handful of Gilles' men, some twenty in number, under the command of Yves de Kersalion, then 'took' the castle. Gilles followed soon after, bringing with him 2,000 *écus* which he gave to Anne de la Suze as an advance on the sum agreed. He had himself received the money from Jean V as an advance. Anne de la Suze then left.

It had been arranged that Jean de Malestroit, the bishop of Nantes, should take possession of the castle in the Duke's name. But before handing the castle over, Gilles had to remove the evidence of his crimes as he had done at Machecoul.

According to the evidence given by Henriet, they only had two days to complete the task before the bishop arrived. There were some forty bodies hidden in a tower. These may be assumed to be corpses of the children who died in the first wave of killing after the death of Jean de Craon. With barely forty-eight hours in hand there was only time to recover the remains, and it would need to be done with more efficiency than at Machecoul. The actual burning of the bones would be a long process and would need to be completed elsewhere. According to Poitou's evidence, Gilles ordered Gilles de Sillé, Hiquet de Brémont, Robin Romulart and Henriet to accompany him

> to the tower of the castle of Champtocé, where the bodies and bones of several dead children were to be found, to take them and put them in strong chests and to transport them to Machecoul; all of which was done. And they found in the said tower the bones of thirty-six or forty-six children, which bones were dried up and he could not remember the exact number. And the chests in which they were placed were bound up with strong rope lest they should break open and the scandal and iniquity of so great a crime should break upon the world.
>
> Questioned on the manner in which he noted the number of bodies he answered that they made a count of the number of heads, but he could not remember the actual number....

The journey to Machecoul was made partly by boat down the Loire. On their arrival they took the remains to Gilles' room and burned them in the presence of Gilles himself, Gilles de Sillé, Henriet, Poitou and the two choristers André Buchet and Rossignol. Hiquet de Brémont and Robin Romulart do not appear to have been present. Then, according to Poitou, 'the dust or ashes of the said children was thrown into the water-pipes of the said castle of Champtocé'.

This time they worked more efficiently, despite the rush, and by the time the bishop arrived there was no trace of any incriminating evidence.

René de la Suze, having made quite sure that the Duke of Brittany bore him no ill will for having occupied Champtocé in the first place, arranged for two of his lawyers, Jean Jehanneau and Geoffroy de la Touche, to collect 4,000 *livres* at Nantes in August; 1,000 *livres* remain unaccounted for under the terms of his agreement with his brother. Perhaps he hoped to receive them when La Mothe-Achard was handed over. At all events, for the moment everyone seemed satisfied.

Yet Gilles' financial problems remained. His transaction with Jean V merely involved the return of mortgaged property equivalent in value to Champtocé and Ingrandes. He received no money, or very little. He still had his chapel to maintain and his lavish generosity continued. Financially he was bleeding himself to death. There was hardly anything left to sell, and the royal edict, ineffectual as it might be in some ways, was none the less still operative in French territory.

He tried to cheat his brother René. He refused to hard over the castle of La Mothe-Achard as agreed, and took Saint-Etienne-de-Mer-Morte, which René had received under the settlement of his grandfather's estate in 1434, by force. There was no comedy siege this time. Gilles was serious. Yet, even if he could raise money on this property once again it would still not be enough. René de la Suze immediately took the matter to law and, by any standards had a strong case. The dispute was settled out of court on January 15 of the following year. Gilles retained Saint-Etienne-de-Mer-Morte. Yet even if he could raise money on this property again it would still not be enough. A constant supply of gold had to be found somewhere.

12

Alchemy and Black Magic

It is not certain when Gilles had his first introduction to the arts of alchemy. Everyone knew of it, of course, in a more or less vague manner and the Church had taken a sufficiently serious view of it to condemn and outlaw its practice. But Gilles had never been over-concerned with the niceties of law, canon or common, and now only magic could save him from disaster. Pampered and spoiled, constantly surrounded by servants who only existed to supply his wants, it seemed logical to him to employ someone to manufacture the money he so badly needed. Besides he had seen the power of the supernatural; he had witnessed divine intervention in human affairs during his brief campaign side by side with Joan. He knew of her secret knowledge. She had spoken of it to d'Alençon and to her judges, as documentary evidence shows. Doubtless she had spoken of it to him as well. Now he, too, needed to make an appeal to the secret powers.

But there was a difference. Whatever connection Joan had with the witch-cult it was entirely moral. In her mind there was a perfect fusion between orthodox Catholicism and the beliefs of the Old Religion. There is no evidence of her ever having exploited her position for her own ends. But with Gilles there was only the search for gratification. By the time he began his experiments in alchemy his mind was so confused and befuddled that everything he touched necessarily turned to corruption. And what in Joan's mind had been perfect unity became split in his own mind into contending factions, so that while turning to magic he was continually obsessed by the salvation of his own soul, jumping in and out of the magic circles, both mentally and physically, and proclaiming his orthodoxy.

At first Gilles merely dabbled. There were attempts to invoke the aid of the devil here and there. The indictment mentions invocations made at Orléans and in Nantes. Gilles mentions having encountered a knight in Angers, who possessed a *grimoire*. In his confession he stated

> That he had received from a certain knight in Anjou, at that time imprisoned for heresy, a certain book on the art of Alchemy, which he had read several times and had had publicly read in Angers, in a certain room before several listeners: that he had spoken with the said knight, then in prison, of the practice of the said art of Alchemy and the evocation of devils: which book he stated he had returned to the said knight, not having kept it for long. ...

This encounter is difficult to date with any certainty. The indictment states that Gilles' crimes, both sexual and heretical, began in 1426 but, as we have seen, this is not entirely reliable. Georges Bataille places the meeting in 1426, when Gilles was indeed in Angers levying troops. However, a more probable date, it seems to me, is 1436, when Gilles was once more in Angers and when his need for knowledge of magic and alchemy was much more pressing. If this date is the correct one we are also able to link the incident with another which occurred at the same time.

Gilles was staying at the 'Lion d'Argent', when a goldsmith who claimed to have some knowledge of alchemy was brought to him. Gilles gave him a silver mark and told him to transmute it into gold.

> [This] the goldsmith promised to do, and locked himself in a room where he got drunk and fell asleep. Gilles found him unconscious and in his rage called him a drunken sot and said that he could expect nothing from him. And the goldsmith left with the silver mark, which the accused lost.

This particular piece of evidence was given by Eustache Blanchet, on 17 October 1440. Blanchet, who was a priest from the Saint-Malo district, was to play an important, if increasingly unwilling rôle in the remaining years of Gilles' life. He was born about 1401 and entered Gilles' service in 1435, presumably as a member of the Chapel of the Holy Innocents. Before long, however, he was being employed to find people with some knowledge of alchemy. As a royal edict was also in force banning the practice, as well as a papal prohibition, doubtless it was felt that it was safer to use a priest as a go-between.

Gilles' knowledge of the magic arts was extremely superficial, despite his brief access to a *grimoire,* but having seen it as his means of salvation his interest became obsessive. At first it was Gilles de Sillé who supplied him with practitioners, just as he had supplied him with his first child victims. The names of some of them survive : Antoine de Palerme, François le Lombard, Thomas Onafrasimus and Dusmenil, known as 'Trompette'. None of them appears to have been successful. Some evocations took place at Machecoul at an unspecified date. In his confession Gilles stated that Dusmenil had told him

> that the Devil, in order to do what the accused intended asking of him, wished to see made and to receive a pact signed by the accused's own hand, in blood from his finger, in which he would promise to give to the Devil, when he came, certain things which he, the accused, could not remember : and for this reason and to this end he signed the said pact with blood from his little finger, in his own name, *Gilles.* As to what was written on the said pact he did not remember, except that he promised the Devil what was stated in the said pact, on condition that the Devil gave him and procured him power and riches.

Asked whether he had offered the Devil his soul, Gilles replied that he was sure he had not. It was something he consistently refused to do. On another occasion a woman was brought to him and told him that he would never be successful unless he abandoned 'a work he had begun or intended to continue'. This presumably referred to his chapel. Again Gilles refused.

Some occasions were not without their comic aspects. One unnamed magician, who was brought to Tiffauges, attempted an evocation in the presence of Gilles and his cousin de Sillé. Both were obviously terrified. The three shut themselves in a lower room of the castle and the magic circle was drawn. De Sillé refused to enter it 'but withdrew towards a window with the intention of jumping out if he felt anything fearful was approaching, and in his arms he held an image of the Blessed

Virgin'. Gilles got as far as stepping inside the circle but he was equally afraid, 'because the magician had forbidden him to make the sign of the cross, for if he should make it they would all be in great danger. But he remembered a prayer to Our Lady which begins *Alma* and straightway the magician ordered him out of the circle, which he did immediately, making the sign of the cross.'

De Sillé appears to have taken this as his cue for a quick exit—he jumped out of the window. Gilles also rushed from the room slamming the door behind him. Some short space of time seems to have elapsed, and when Gilles saw de Sillé again he was told that 'someone was beating the said magician who had been left alone in the room and it sounded as though someone were beating a feather mattress'. When he listened outside the door Gilles could hear nothing. On opening it he found 'the magician, wounded in the face and in other parts of his body, and having, among other things, a big lump on his forehead ... so hurt that he could hardly stand up; and he was afraid he might die of these wounds and asked that he might make confession and receive the holy sacraments; but the magician did not die and recovered from his wounds'.

This has all the marks of a comedy carefully staged for Gilles' benefit. However, other magicians de Sillé found did genuinely come to grief. One was drowned on his way to the castle and another died almost immediately on arrival. These incidents were not without their effect on Gilles. He regarded them as a sign and a warning, 'and for this reason he intended giving up his wicked life and making a pilgrimage to Jerusalem and to the Holy Sepulchre and to other places of the Passion of Our Saviour, and to do all he could to obtain the remission of his sins through the mercy and compassion of his Saviour'.

This was the first of many moments of self-examination and doubt, and the first indication that he was assailed by feelings of depression and guilt. This resolution to make a pilgrimage was renewed many times, as Blanchet testified, but like so much else it remained a dream.

De Sillé appears to have had enough by now for it was Blanchet who found the next magician, Jean de la Rivière, who came from Poitiers. On Gilles' instructions Blanchet brought him to Pouzauges where he was instructed to summon the Devil. Blanchet gave the following account of one attempt:

> One night, dressed in white armour and armed with a sword and other weapons, he came to a wood situated near the said place of Pouzauges; and the said accused, Etienne Corillaut, Henriet and the witness himself accompanied him to the said wood; and the said La Rivière left the above mentioned at the edge of the said wood and went in alone to make the said evocations as he had promised and the present witness and the others waited.

A great clanging was then heard which Blanchet frankly thought was La Rivière beating his own armour, although he said nothing at the time. La Rivière then emerged from the wood and Gilles asked him if anything important had occurred.

> The said La Rivière, making as though he were afraid and greatly troubled in his mind, said he had seen a demon in the shape of a leopard and it had passed close by him, disdaining to look at him and refusing to speak to him or say anything at all. La Rivière gave the accused Gilles little reason for this.
>
> After this the aforesaid Gilles, La Rivière and the others went to Pouzauges where they indulged in many pleasures and then slept.

Whatever Blanchet's private doubts may have been, Gilles was evidently convinced by this performance, and La Rivière capitalised on his advantage before it was too late.

> The next day, the said La Rivière claimed that he needed certain necessary things for his evocations and the said accused, Gilles, gave him 20 *écus* or *réaux* and asked him to obtain whatever was necessary for the undertaking and to return without delay, which he promised to do. And he went away and never returned to the said Gilles to the witness's best knowledge or from what he has heard.

Despite this further disappointment Gilles was not prepared to give up. For one thing he could not afford to; for another he only recognised his own necessity, not the limitations of the outer world.

Early in 1439, Blanchet, who was not yet a permanent member of Gilles' household but, according to his own evidence, merely attached to it, was obliged to go to Italy on business. The exact nature of this business was never specified. Italy at this time was reputed to be the centre of alchemic knowledge, and Blanchet was accordingly instructed to find a first-class practitioner and bring him back. The precise date of his departure was not known but it is reasonable to allow three or four months for the journey and he was back by the end of April 1439. He probably left Tiffauges in January of that year.

Having presumably attended to his own affairs, Blanchet arrived in Florence, where he made the acquaintance of Guglielmo di Montepulciano, Nicolò de' Medici and Francesco di Vastellane, all of whom practised the art of alchemy. After a short time they introduced him to François Prelati, a clerk in minor orders. At the trial in 1440 he testified that 'he was born in Montecatini in the Val di Nievole, near Pistoia, in the diocese of Luca, in Italy, that he was a clerk, having received the tonsure from the Bishop of Arezzo, having studied poetry, geomancy, and other arts and sciences, in particular alchemy. He thought he was about twenty-three years old.' At the time Blanchet met him he was in the service of the Bishop of Mondovi.

Blanchet proceeded with caution, first cultivating his friendship and then slowly broaching the business in hand. Blanchet was evidently satisfied with him, and Prelati, who had gathered what information he could, allowed himself to be drawn slowly. Perhaps not least among Prelati's qualifications was the fact that he was young and handsome and would be physically pleasing to Gilles. He spoke elegant Latin and French and seemed generally cultivated. As for his other attributes, he stated in evidence later at the trial that he had been initiated into the arts of alchemy and evocation by Jean de Fontenelle, a French doctor living in Florence. This was in 1437. Fontenelle on one occasion succeeded in invoking twenty crows in the upper room of his house. On another occasion he managed to invoke a demon called Barron, who appeared as a young man. Prelati made a pact with him, promising him a chicken, a dove, or a pigeon each time he appeared.

Having learned this, Blanchet began to sound Prelati out more closely.

This same Eustache [Blanchet] asked him if he would like to go to France. To which the said François [Prelati] replied that he had a cousin called de Martellis who lived in Nantes in Brittany and that he would be happy to go and see him.... Then the said Eustache told this same François that there lived in France a man of great position, to wit the Baron de Rais, who greatly desired to have a man versed in the said arts in his household and that if the said François was so versed and wished to come and live with the said lord, he would receive generous treatment from him.

Prelati agreed at once. No doubt Blanchet had given his Florentine acquaintances some idea of the extravagant manner of life which Gilles led and this would have been more than sufficient inducement. Blanchet and Prelati set off immediately 'and the said witness [Prelati] took with him, from Florence, a book dealing with evocations and the art of Alchemy'.

Eventually Blanchet and Prelati arrived at Saint-Florent-le Vieil, south of the Loire, where they stayed for some days. Blanchet wrote to Gilles informing him of the success of his mission. Gilles immediately despatched Henriet and Poitou, accompanied by two other unnamed men, to bring them to Tiffauges. Gilles was evidently delighted with Blanchet's account of Prelati's qualifications and was anxious to set him to work as quickly as possible. Blanchet was then invited to take up residence at the castle, an offer about which he had mixed feelings but which he could not refuse. Blanchet, Prelati, Jean Petit, a goldsmith brought especially from Paris, and an old woman named Perrotte, all shared the same room. This presumably was to keep them apart from the rest of the household and prevent gossip.

Prelati had not travelled all the way from Italy for nothing. He soon realised how greatly he was needed and was also aware that no one could dispute his expert knowledge or call his competence into question. He was clever and entirely without scruple and it did not take him long to establish a complete ascendancy, both intellectual and, one suspects, sexual, over his new master.

Work began immediately in earnest. Experiments were made daily and even the sceptical Blanchet appears to have taken them seriously. Prelati attempted to invoke the aid of his particular demon, Barron. At first only Gilles and Prelati were present during the ceremonies. Blanchet gives the following account:

> Gilles used to arrive in the said room, sometimes during the night, sometimes during the day, sometimes even at cock-crow. And after Gilles' arrival 'he, the witness, and Perrotte would leave the room and leave the said François and Gilles together.

Gilles used to give them accounts of what happened later.

> Another day, the witness saw the accused Gilles and François go into a lower room, behind the one in which the witness and the others used to pass the night and ... stay there for some time. Then the witness heard the said François say the following words, among others, in a low voice: 'Come then Satan' or 'Come You'. The witness believes that this same François added the words 'to our aid' but he knows nothing more. And the said François uttered several other words which the witness could not hear clearly and that he is not able to report. The said Gilles and François remained there for about half an hour with the candle alight. And shortly after these words were spoken a cold wind blew suddenly through the castle.

No more tangible sign of the devil's presence was forthcoming.

For the time being Prelati was unaware, or so he claimed at the trial, of Gilles' sexual crimes. He was informed later by one of the servants, Guillaume Daussy. There was no reason why he should have been let into the secret. It is essential to realise that Gilles' paedophilia and homicide were quite distinct from his alchemic and satanic practices. They coexist but they do not connect. There is no evidence that Gilles ever indulged in human sacrifice, although he did later supply parts of the bodies of his victims for Prelati's ceremonies. Gilles would have continued to abuse and murder children whatever the circumstances. Only financial necessity made him indulge in demonic practices.

Shortly after his arrival Prelati made contact with a local

alchemist whom he described as a 'dyed-in-the-wool Breton', and who was living 'in the house of Geoffroy Leconte, captain of the said castle [Tiffauges]. He was treating the captain's wife for a disease of the eyes. The witness [Prelati] found a leather-bound book, partly of paper, partly of parchment, with writing in it and headings and rubrics in red. Now this book contained evocations of demons and various other questions concerning medicine, astrology and others.' Prelati succeeded in borrowing it and showed it, together with the one he had brought from Italy, to Gilles, who decided that they would experiment with the matter contained in them.

One evening, after supper, Gilles, Prelati, de Sillé, Blanchet, Henriet and Poitou made preparations for what was evidently to be the most serious attempt at an evocation that had been made since Prelati arrived in April. Poitou, in his evidence, stated that 'Prelati ... made a great circle in the hall of the castle of Tiffauges with the point of a sword. And he made crosses, signs and characters, like armorial bearings, in the four parts of the said circle.'

Poitou, Henriet and Blanchet were then ordered to bring

a great quantity of coal, incense, a magnetic stone ... an earthen pot, torches, candlesticks, fire and other things ... which the said Gilles and Prelati arranged in certain parts of the said circle: and a great fire was lit in the pot which had coal in it. Then the said François made other signs or characters, still like armorial bearings, near and on the wall of the room, in the angle of the door: and he lit another fire near the signs he had just made. And immediately after that the said François opened the four windows of the said hall which was in the form or manner of a cross.

After these preparations had been made, Gilles ordered everyone except François and himself from the room, swearing them to secrecy. Prelati gave an account of what followed:

The said Gilles and the present witness placed themselves in the middle of the circles and in a certain angle near the wall in which the present witness traced another character. There were burning coals in the earthen pot; on which coals they put magnetic powder, incense and aloes from which a stinking smoke arose. And they stayed there, sometimes standing, sometimes sitting, sometimes kneeling so that they might adore the demons and make sacrifices to them, for almost two hours, invoking demons, making all efforts to invoke them diligently, the said Gilles and the present witness reading in turns from the said book, waiting for the demon they had invoked to appear but ... nothing appeared on that occasion.

The book they read from, according to Prelati, stated

that demons had the power to reveal hidden treasure, to teach philosophy and to guide those who were active in the world. The words he used in his invocations were as follows: 'I conjure you Barron, Satan, Beelzebub, Belial, in the name of the Father, the Son and the Holy Ghost, in the name of the Virgin Mary and all the saints, to appear in person, to speak with us and do our will.'

The confusion of demonolgy and orthodox theology is worth noting here.

Gilles, as it would appear from his evidence, held a pact written in his own hand and bearing his signature. He had prepared this beforehand on Prelati's instructions. He was to hand it over if Prelati and the devil could arrive at a satisfactory agreement.

Those who had been excluded from the ceremony were listening outside. They could hear Prelati's voice but could not distinguish precisely what he was saying. Then they heard, according to Henriet; 'a certain noise, like that of a four-legged animal walking on the roof, approaching the skylight of the pond where they kept fish in the said place, near the room in which the said Gilles and François were to be found.'

All probability no more than a cat trying to get at the fish, but in the over-heated and near-hysterical atmosphere that reigned at Tiffauges they may well have imagined it was the leopard Jean de la Rivière claimed to have seen.

From all accounts Gilles and Prelati attempted invocations every day for five weeks, but never with any success. One such was made the evening after the events just described. This time Gilles decided upon an experiment in the open air. He sent Prelati and Poitou, according to the latter's own evidence, 'to a small field, a quarter of a league distant from Tiffauges in the direction of Montaign.'

Gilles' absence is most probably explained by the bad weather that night. He had given Prelati another pact, or perhaps the one from the previous night, bearing the words; 'Come to my aid and I will give you all you desire, except my soul and the abridgement of my life.'

Poitou was not at all happy about being sent and did his best to persuade Gilles to excuse him, but to no purpose. Prelati assured him there would be no danger. The proceedings themselves were more or less a repetition of the previous night's ceremonies.

When they arrived at the field the said François made a circle with the aid of a knife with crosses and characters, as he had done in the room in the castle. And having set light to the coals the said François forbade the witness to make the sign of the cross and enjoined him to step inside the circle as he himself did. And both of them being in the circle, the said François made his invocations.

Poitou, apparently, could make nothing of what was said although he did pick out the name Barron. He also made the sign of the cross, without Prelati's noticing. They continued their efforts for about half an hour in a torrential shower of rain, then gave up. It was so dark that they could hardly find their way back. They were unable to get into the castle as the gate had been closed for the night and to wake the guard might arouse suspicion and lead to awkward questions. They put up in a house in the village where Blanchet was waiting for them. Beds had been prepared for them all and a good fire laid. They had had a soaking for nothing. The night had been a typical failure.

13

Jean V

Echoes of Gilles' earlier public life were still heard. In the early summer of 1439 he came into contact with Jeanne des Amboises who had been claiming consistently since 1436 that she was Joan of Arc. One popular legend had always maintained that Joan had not been burned at all but had been miraculously saved. Jeanne des Amboises had travelled through Germany and France and, somewhat surprisingly, had been accepted by Joan's brothers as their real sister. Possibly they were trying to recoup some of the wealth and privilege they had enjoyed during Joan's lifetime.

Gilles, too, accepted her for a while. He allotted her a number of troops whom he placed under the command of Jean de Siquenville. He had no intention of campaigning himself. Those days were over. An expedition to relieve Le Mans was considered but did not come to anything. Gilles went through a certain number of motions with this new Joan but he tired of her very quickly. There were rumours that Charles VII had exposed her as a fraud when she was unable to repeat the secret Joan had revealed to him at Chinon ten years earlier, and Gilles himself had known the real Joan so well that this new girl could not deceive him for long. And perhaps, for once, he was not prepared to deceive himself. Besides, the experience he had shared with Joan was past and he had written it off shortly after her capture. The masquerade itself did not last. In 1440 the girl admitted her deception and disappeared into Italy.

All this was merely a brief interlude in the much more serious business of the transmutation of base metals into gold. And Prelati still had to live up to his promises. Gilles was infatuated with him sexually, but he was still demanding gold and Prelati had to invent fresh possibilities and arouse fresh hopes. They considered a new method of invocation involving a crested bird and a dyadrous stone but as the requisite stone was not obtainable they had to abandon the idea. The experiments continued on the same basis as before, but Prelati managed to persuade Gilles to stay away. How he managed this it is impossible to say, but it may well be he suggested that as Gilles was not willing to commit himself totally, without the reservations concerning his soul, there was no purpose in his attending. Indeed his presence might well be a hindrance.

Gilles agreed, and no sooner was Prelati left to practise on his own than Barron appeared some ten or twelve times 'in the form of a handsome young man of about twenty-five, wearing a red or violet cloak'. Prelati knew how attractive this image would be to Gilles and he may well have taken the part himself.

At some time during July and August Gilles went to Bourges. The reason for the visit is unknown. He left instructions with Prelati that he was to continue his experiments and send word of any results. Shortly afterwards he received a silver vessel with unguent in it, which was carried in a small purse. He also received a silver box which contained a piece of slate with some black powder on it. These were supposedly gifts from Barron. Prelati gave them to de Sillé, who entrusted them to Gascard de Pouzauges to take to Gilles in Bourges. Gilles wore the purse round his neck for some time on the promise that it would bring him prosperity, but finding it apparently no use he got rid of it. One version has it that he threw the purse down the well of the old house of Jacques Coeur* but this does not coincide with evidence given later at the trial, when Poitou maintained it was returned to Prelati.

When Gilles returned from Bourges, Prelati staged an elaborate performance for his benefit.

> [He] made an invocation in the said hall at Tiffauges, where Barron appeared in human form; and the witness [Prelati] asked money of him in the name of Messire de Rais. And shortly after, indeed, he saw in a room what seemed like a great quantity of gold in ingots; which gold remained there for some days; as soon as he saw it the witness desired to touch it and the evil spirit answered that he should not

*Not the present Palais de Jacques Coeur

because it was not yet time. All which the witness reported
to the said Gilles; and this same Messire Gilles asked him if
he might see it and if it was allowed; to which the witness
replied, 'Yes'; and they both went to the said room and as
they entered a huge snake strong and with wings, about the
size of a dog, appeared on the floor and the witness told the
said Gilles not to enter because of the serpent he had seen;
much afraid the said Gilles ran away and the witness followed.
after which the said Messire Gilles took a cross in which there
were fragments of the true cross, so that he might enter the
room with greater security; but the witness told him that it
was no good to use a blessed cross in such matters. Shortly
after the witness entered the said room and when he touched
the seeming gold he saw that it was nothing but a tawny-
coloured powder and thus he knew the falseness of the evil
spirit.

Whatever else he may have been, Prelati was a first-class
showman, able to build up expectations, let them down in a
convincing way and find an appropriate excuse. He had to
exercise a great deal of ingenuity to keep his place, which he
would not willingly have relinquished.

According to Blanchet, Prelati received a thorough beating
from the demon on one occasion. He states that Gilles sent for
him from the village and that when he arrived he found the
Baron de Rais in a highly depressed state because he thought
François was dead.

[Blanchet] had heard him [Gilles] making a great clamour in
the room in the castle where he lived and he had heard the
sound of blows *as though someone were beating a feather
bed,* but that he had not gone into the said room and begged
the witness to go and see what was happening. But the
witness said he dare not go in either. None the less, to please
the said Gilles, the witness went to the said room but did not
go in, but as the room had an opening, high up, he called
the said François Prelati through it but he did not answer. The
witness heard him moan with pain like a man severely
wounded; all which he reported to the said Gilles who was
much distressed by it. Then the said François came out, looking
very pale, and went to the room of the said Gilles; and he

recounted that the devil had beaten him horribly in the said room. As a result of this chastisement, the said François had a fever and was ill for seven or eight days. And the accused Gilles looked after the said François entirely, during his illness, not allowing anyone else to care for him; and he had him shriven and the said François recovered from his illness. [Emphasis added.]

This may be an accurate account, and has certainly been accepted as such by other biographers, but it is open to doubt. First, neither Gilles nor Prelati mentions it in his evidence, which, in other respects, is fairly complete. Secondly Blanchet is unable to give an accurate date for it. He says it occurred when he was 'in the town of Tiffauges, not within the castle of the said place, and it was not the time when he lodged in the castle'. Now he lived in the castle from Prelati's arrival on Ascension Day, May 12, until All Saints Day, 1439, and did not return to Tiffauges again after that date. He also says 'that he went to the castle to meet clerics and on other matters.' This was his situation in 1438. It seems more than possible that Blanchet is confusing Prelati with the other unnamed alchemist who was severely beaten. One or two circumstantial details would seem to confirm this view. First, the sound 'as though someone were beating a feather bed', which occurs in the earlier incident. Secondly the duration of the illness and the administration of the last rites. The suggestion by Michel Bataille that Prelati re-staged an earlier incident seems to me to pay insufficient credit to his ingenuity and intelligence. He may well have been ill at some time and been devotedly nursed by Gilles, causing Blanchet to confuse two separate incidents.

Gilles became more and more dependent on his magician-alchemist, relying on his advice in practically everything. In August he went, with Prelati and his entire household, to Bourgneuf-en-Rais to meet Jean V. There seems to have been no particular reason for this visit except a desire to ensure that the Duke would take him 'into his good grace'. He stayed at the convent of the Frères Mineurs and while there asked Prelati to invoke his devils to make certain he would have a favourable reception from the Duke. He felt frightened suddenly and needed reassurance. None was forthcoming.

However much Gilles tried to live in his private universe and pretend that the world did not exist, he was aware that his own safety and well-being depended on what he had to offer; and that now was almost nothing. His family were unremitting in their campaign to try to dispossess him; he had virtually nothing left to sell and Jean V had achieved his ambition to become master of Champtocé. The Duke had no further reason to maintain his friendship with a man on the way to financial ruin, whose habits and practices were notorious throughout large parts of the country.

For once Gilles' political instincts were right. At some date which is difficult to determine, Jean V joined forces with the Bishop of Nantes, Jean de Malestroit, who had been on bad terms with Gilles since the fiasco of Saint-James-de-Beuvron in 1427, and began to engineer Gilles' downfall. The Duke was aware of Gilles' reputation. He was not concerned on moral grounds. The deaths of a few, or even a few hundred children more or less made no difference to him. They were so much clutter. However if Gilles could be branded as a criminal it would provide an excuse for confiscating all his lands within the Duchy. Malestroit began discreetly collecting information until a convenient time could be found to make use of it.

Despite his apprehension and his desire to maintain good relations with the Duke, Gilles could not control his erotic drives. He once told Poitou that no one would ever understand what he did, but that his star drove him to it. Before meeting Jean V at Bourgneuf, he stopped at the Hotel de la Suze, in Nantes. His first victim was Colin Avril, aged about eighteen or twenty, rather older than Gilles' usual victims but apparently young-looking.

Later that month he moved to Bourgneuf where he stayed at the convent. On the 25th another boy, Bernard le Camus, was brought to him.

A fit of depression followed these incidents and Gilles' meeting with the Duke. Perhaps Jean V was not as cordial as he might have been. At all events, according to Blanchet, Gilles talked of reform, of changing his ways and making a pilgrimage to the Holy Land. But the mood was short-lived. On the 28th Jean Toutblanc, a thirteen-year-old boy, disappeared and in October two sons of Robin Pavot were lost. Doubtless all the people in

Gilles' entourage did their best to revive their master's spirits.

In the meantime the experiments and invocations continued, with increasing desperation, one imagines. It is difficult to see how Gilles was maintaining his household. He had a few properties left but the income from them would not have been anywhere near sufficient. He urged his new friend, Prelati, to greater efforts. Prelati on his side had to find new excuses for his continued lack of success. He claimed that Barron had told him that if Gilles 'would give food to three poor men in his name at three great feasts in the year' then success would be his. Gilles complied on All Saints Day but did not follow through on subsequent occasions, thus giving Prelati a perfect excuse to explain away his failure.

It was at All Saints that Blanchet decided the time had come to go. According to his own evidence, he had a discussion with Robin Romulart. He claimed he was appalled by the idea that Prelati was working with devils and said that he had decided to leave. Few in Gilles' household would have been deceived by this excuse. Whether Blanchet, being a cleric, had heard rumours that Jean de Malestroit was collecting evidence is uncertain, but certainly he seems to have decided that it was no longer safe to be found in Gilles' entourage. He went to Montagne and stayed with a man named Bouchard-Menard.

Blanchet was right in his assessment of the situation. Gilles may have been apprehensive about the Duke of Brittany but he was so turned in upon himself, so dominated by the smooth-talking Prelati, that he could not see the wider political changes that were taking place in France. Charles VII, once the despised and slighted Dauphin, had grown in assurance with the years. After a meeting of the Estates General in Orléans in October, to which Gilles, although a Marshal of France, was not even invited, Charles decided to form a regular army, one that would be subject to royal authority alone, one, above all, that would deal effectively with rebellious and fractious nobles like Gilles. In this he was assisted by his son the future Louis XI, perhaps the most devious and ruthless monarch France has ever known, who also needed to be kept under a tight control. Gilles, according to the scant evidence available, still made the occasional raid on the English but this was mere banditry and just the sort of activity which the king regarded with increasing suspicion and displeasure. A long struggle was beginning now between an increasingly centralised government and an aristocracy which was trying to hold on to its feudal privileges. No one could have represented this aristocracy more vividly than Gilles.

If times had changed since the campaign of 1429, Gilles had not changed with them. He knew no laws—it was years since he had performed his duties as Marshal adequately; he had taken money under false pretences, attacked the king's mother-in-law and terrorised the countryside. He still pursued his private feuds in the mediaeval manner. He fought with Jean de Harpedenne and also the captain in charge of the garrison at Palluau, whom he suspected of preparing a raid on Saint-Etienne-de-Mer-Morte. He tried to set up an ambush but Prelati informed him that Barron had foretold they would not meet up with the enemy that day. For once he told the truth and Gilles was greatly disappointed.

At the beginning of December 1439 Gilles was given tangible evidence of the change in the political climate. He received a visit from the Dauphin Louis, who had been sent by his father to put an end to the pillaging and private wars in Poitou. Charles also hoped by this means to prevent his son from forming an alliance with the dissident nobles.

The Dauphin visited Pouzauges and Tiffauges. Before he arrived at Tiffauges Gilles had all trace of his experiments removed. Louis was sharp-eyed and entirely without pity. If he found anything that was outside the law he would not hesitate to use it. Precious retorts, vessels and other equipment were smashed and the debris hidden, all evidence of traffic with the devil was destroyed. It must have been a panic akin to the two days when they removed all the bodies from Machecoul.

On his arrival at Tiffauges Louis immediately arrested Jean de Siquenville, whom Gilles had entrusted with troops to support the pseudo Joan of Arc. He was little better than a bandit, living off the countryside. Louis had him thrown into the dungeons of Montaign. But de Siquenville, in himself, was not important. His arrest was much more of a warning to Gilles that firm action would be taken in the future against those who disobeyed royal commands.

Gilles took the warning to heart. He knew now what to expect from the king of France. De Siquenville managed to escape and some time later obtain a pardon, but to Gilles the wisest move seemed to be to move to Brittany where the Duke, nominally at least, was his friend and where he still enjoyed the title of Lieutenant-General. He moved with his household to Machecoul.

He was also worried by Blanchet's absence. He had been gone seven weeks and showed no sign of returning. About the time of Louis the Dauphin's visit, Blanchet was visited by Jean Mercier, who had charge of the castle of La Roche-sur-Yon. He asked him for news. Mercier told him that rumours were spreading. It was being openly said that Gilles was a child murderer and was practising magic. The local populace had no idea of the nature of Gilles' sexual crimes. They imagined that he was writing a great book in his own hand with the blood of the children he had killed. When the book was complete he would then have the power to take any stronghold he wished and he would be invulnerable. Gilles was already becoming the ogre of fairy tale and the foundations of future legends were being laid.

This conversation confirmed Blanchet's suspicions. The following day Jean Petit, the goldsmith, arrived with a message from Gilles. He was to return at once. Blanchet refused. He warned Petit about the rumours and the gossip. In his opinion Gilles and Prelati should stop at once. On his return Petit repeated this conversation to Gilles and was thrown into the dungeon at Saint-Etienne-de-Mer-Morte for his pains. He remained there for some considerable time.

Gilles realised that Blanchet fully intended to desert and that not only did he know too much but he was unable to keep his mouth shut. A few days after Petit's return he sent de Sillé, Poitou, Henriet and Jean Lebreton to take Blanchet by force. This was on about December 20. He was to be taken to Saint-Etienne-de-Mer-Morte, where he would be put into a dungeon and left to rot. Blanchet was taken without difficulty and the journey began. At Roche-Servière he refused to go any farther. He persuaded his captors to take him to Machecoul, where Gilles was now in residence, and seems to have managed to persuade him to adopt a more moderate attitude. He was allowed to live in the village in the house of Perrot Colin. Perhaps Gilles had decided that an unwilling accomplice was better than no accomplice at all. Prelati, who had been lodging with the Marchese de Ceva, one of Gilles' military establishment, was sent to keep an eye on him.

Before moving in with Blanchet, Prelati gave proof of the petty viciousness of his nature. He and de Ceva occupied an upper room in the house of Perrine Rondeau and her husband in the village of Machecoul. Clément Rondeau was thought to be dying and was given extreme unction. Perrine was in tears and went to sit in Prelati's room. Prelati and de Ceva had gone to the castle leaving their pages behind to have their supper. On their return they were enraged to find Perrine in their room. They insulted her, then took her by the feet and shoulders intending to throw her down the ladder which led to the lower room which she occupied. Prelati kicked her in the backside to send her on her way and had the nurse not caught her by the skirts she would have crashed to the floor.

*   *   *   *

The murders continued. About December 10, before Blanchet returned, Jeanette Drouet sent her children aged 10 and 7 to beg for alms at Machecoul. They were never seen again.

About Christmas-time Ysabeau Hamelin lost two children, one of fifteen and the other of seven. She sent them to buy bread in Machecoul but they never returned. The next day Prelati and the Marchese de Ceva, whom she knew by sight, arrived at the house. A curious conversation then ensued of which she gave details in her evidence:

> The Marchese asked her if her breast was cured. She answered by asking him how he knew she had been ill, for in point of fact she had not. He said that she had, then he told her she was not a local woman but from Pouancé. She acknowledged the truth of this. Thereupon he glanced inside the house and asked her if she had a husband, and she answered yes but he had gone back to their own part of the world to see if there was any work there. And as he noticed two children in the house he asked her if they were hers; to which she replied that she had two others, but did not mention the

fact that they had disappeared, because she dared not speak about it. Then they went away, and as they went away she heard the Marchese say to François that two had come out of that house.

Just over a week previously Ysabeau had heard of the disappearance of a child belonging to Micheau Bouer. She must have had a good idea of what had happened to her own children. Perhaps she had imagined that by sending two together, one of them an older boy, they would be safe. But there were no safeguards for people in her position. Prelati's and de Ceva's visit, with its conversational preliminaries, was obviously designed to see if she would mention the disappearance and to warn her against doing so.

Anxiety was beginning to be felt at the castle, if not by Gilles at least by his companions. There was nowhere else they could go now. They had moved into a corner from which there was no escape.

14

The Final Madness

The reality which Gilles had tried so desperately to exclude had slowly and inevitably been taking its revenge. In fact his perfect world had lasted but two years. By the time he left Orléans in 1435 he was virtually ruined. Everything had gone downhill ever since. Once he had been able to change his residence as easily as he changed his clothes; now he felt safe only at Machecoul. All he had to look forward to was the same, endless grubbing for money, the endless setting off of one debt against another, the endlessly futile experiments and invocations, with not a speck of gold to show for them, the endless abuse and slaughter of children.

However much he may have tried to suppress the knowledge, he was aware that his world was disintegrating for the third time. The signs were unmistakable. This time he had even less to fall back on; the first time there had been his grandfather, the second time there had been his wealth, this time he had nothing but a collection of parasites who might or might not stay with him if circumstances became really difficult.

The depressions which he had been experiencing increased in intensity. They were accompanied, as usual, by an access of religious sentiment. At Easter he made a rather theatrical appearance at the church of the Holy Trinity at Machecoul. On Easter day, March 27, Blanchet saw him making his confession to Olivier de Ferrières. He then received the sacraments among the poor of the town. They tried to stand aside out of respect for his position, but he waved them forward to receive the bread and wine from the officiating priest, Simon Loisel, before him. It was a perfect display of humble piety. How deep it went is another question. How full had his confession been? Did he really spell out all his crimes to Olivier de Ferrières?

If he did not his confession was valueless, and he knew it. And by going on to receive the sacraments he had committed one more mortal sin. Yet he made the gesture. Perhaps, in spite of all, he hoped that God would, in some magical way, save him.

The mood passed. He returned to his old habits like a dog to its vomit. By Whitsun, which fell on May 15, there were two more recorded murders. More and more Gilles was buffeted by contradictory impulses which surged up uncontrollably inside him.

The urgency of his situation now forced him into the most overtly senseless act of his entire career. He decided to repossess the castle of Saint-Etienne-de-Mer-Mortè, which he had recently sold to Geoffroy Le Ferron, treasurer to Jean V. The castle was one of which he was particularly fond, if only to keep his prisoners in. It was, moreover, only lightly guarded. Having once taken it away from his brother with impunity, perhaps he imagined he could do the same again. In the past whenever everything else had failed he had always tried banditry. Mostly he had been successful.

The keys to the castle were held by Jean le Ferron, Geoffroy's brother, and officiating priest at Saint-Etienne. He was responsible for the castle during his brother's absence. Gilles rode out with about sixty men, whom he posted in the wood surrounding the church. They then waited until mass was over and the congregation had dispersed. There were still a few members of the congregation inside the church when Gilles burst in, brandishing a double-edged battle-axe and shouting : 'You thieving scoundrels, you have beaten my men and extorted money from them. Come outside the church or I'll lay you out dead!'

This was pure nonsense but it is worth noting that in his excitement Gilles attributed his own crimes to someone else. Le Ferron fell on his knees and begged De Ceva and Bertrand Poulein, who were present, to intercede for him. Both claimed in their testimony that they had done so, but Jean Rousseau, one of the Duke of Brittany's men who was present at the incident, does not mention it. Le Ferron left the church of his own free will, according to De Ceva and Poulein, but Rousseau maintained that he was dragged out. According to his own account Rousseau made a move to defend the priest but was warned off by a gesture from one of Gilles' men. A short while after, he was set upon by Gilles' men and disarmed, presumably as a warning to keep his mouth shut. As for Le Ferron he was thrown into a dungeon as soon as Gilles had taken possession of the castle.

This insane outburst at Whitsun is in strange contrast to the attitude of humble piety displayed at Easter, yet Gilles kept on repeating that he would make a pilgrimage to the Holy Land. Perhaps he thought the mere repetition of a promise would suffice to hold off divine wrath.

By his action Gilles provided Jean with just the pretext he had been waiting for. By marching into the church he had violated ecclesiastical property, by imprisoning a priest he had offended against church law, by dispossessing Geoffroy Le Ferron he had attacked a member of the Duke's household and consequently the Duke himself, and above all, he had transgressed against the rights of feudal possession. Jean V and his Chancellor, Jean de Malestroit, Bishop of Nantes, were now free to move against him.

The Duke imposed on him a fine of 50,000 *écus*. It was crippling. He knew that Gilles could not possibly pay it. His property, such as it was, was consequently forfeit. All the lands he had regained through the sale of Champtocé would be lost again. He would have nothing left but Tiffauges and Pouzauges, which officially belonged to his wife. Everything he had inherited had disappeared. In June, knowing that he could not pay the fine, Gilles moved his prisoner back into French territory and incarcerated him in Tiffauges. In the meantime Jean de Malestroit ordered an official enquiry and began to collect evidence from people who had lost children.

Gilles knew nothing of the investigations that were being made but his own sense of self-preservation caused him to seek another meeting with the Duke, who was the only man who could offer him any kind of protection. Jean V was staying at the time at Josselin and Gilles decided to join him there. Some accommodation must be possible between them. He seemed to have forgotten that whereas in the past he had something to offer, land or military aid, now he had nothing.

He was far from confident of the outcome. Before leaving Machecoul he asked Prelati to consult Barron, to discover if he 'could go to my lord the Duke and return in all security; to which Barron replied "Yes" '. They went through the same ritual at Nantes and again on their arrival at Josselin, where the invocations were made in a field. Gilles was not present, so that Prelati was able to report that Barron had appeared, this time dressed in a violet cloak. Previous reassurances were repeated: Gilles would return safely from the journey. His entourage were told that the object of the journey was to collect money owing from the Duke but none of them was taken in by this story.

There is no record of the Duke's meeting with Gilles. They can have had little to say to each other apart from a conventional exchange of platitudes. Jean V was no longer interested in compromise, his aim was total destruction. The only known incident that occurred during the stay at Josselin is that Henriet took three children to a field and killed them. Presumably it was safe to assault them sexually in the town but not to dispose of them.

On the return journey Gilles decided to spend a short while at Vannes in order to see André Buchet who had left his service and joined the Duke's chapel at a date which it is impossible to fix. Gilles knew that Buchet could supply him with a child. He lodged, discreetly, outside the town in a village called la Mothe, in the house of a man named Lemoine, which was near the Bishop's palace. There Buchet brought him a boy aged about ten. The child was sexually assaulted. However Lemoine's house did not have a room private enough to kill the boy in. He was therefore taken to the house of a man called Bretden where Gilles' squires were lodged. His head was then cut off and burned. The headless corpse was then tied up with the boy's own belt and dropped into the cess-pool in the house. Unfortunately for the murderers, it was still partly visible and Poitou had to be lowered down, with some difficulty, to push it under. Poitou claimed that Buchet was present during the entire proceedings.

At this moment, on July 29, Jean de Malestroit published his findings in the form of letters patent.

> To all those who shall see these present letters, we, Jean, by the divine authority and grace of the Holy Apostolic See, Bishop of Nantes, give greetings in the name of Our Saviour and require you to take note of these present letters.

We make known by these letters that, visiting the parish of
Sainte-Marie in Nantes, in which Gilles de Rais, hereunder
mentioned, frequently resides, in the house known as de la
Suze, and is a parishioner of the said church; and visiting
other parish churches hereunder designated, frequent and
public clamour first reached our ears, then the complaints and
declarations of persons of good character and discretion.

There follows a list of witnesses whose testimony has already
been quoted.

We, visiting these same churches, as it touches our office, have
had them diligently examined and by their depositions have
learned among other things, which we hold for certain, that
the nobleman, Gilles de Rais, knight, lord of the said place
and Baron, our subject and answerable to our laws, with
certain of his accomplices had slaughtered, murdered and
massacred in the most odious fashion several young boys, and
that he had taken with these children pleasure against nature
and practised the vice of sodomy, which he did oftentimes,
and oftentimes had caused invocations of the devil to be
made, to whom he had made sacrifice and with whom he
made a pact and that he had perpetrated other great crimes
within the limits of our jurisdiction; and we have learned
by the enquiries of our commissioners and procurers that the
said Gilles had committed the above-mentioned crimes and
other kinds of debauch in our diocese and in divers other
places dependent upon it.

In respect of which crimes the said Gilles found and still
finds himself in error against grave and honourable personages.
And so that none may have any doubt in the matter we have
written these present letters and caused our seal to be attached
thereunto.

Given at Nantes, 29 July 1440. By order of the said Lord
Bishop of Nantes.

Signed, Jean Petit.*

Much of the material in this letter is familiar but one point
needs clarification. The question of human sacrifice has always
caught the imagination of those studying the life of Gilles de

* Not to be confused with Jean Petit, the goldsmith.

Rais and obviously fascinated those who tried him. There is however only one record of human remains being offered as part of Prelati's invocations. According to Henriet, the original suggestion came from Blanchet, although we cannot be certain if this is true. According to Henriet again, Poitou took the hand and heart of a child, which had been placed in a glass and covered with a cloth, and left it on the chimney-piece of the room where Gilles and Prelati made their invocations. This was some time towards the end of 1439. Whether the child was specifically killed for this purpose or whether the limbs were taken from one of Gille's other victims we do not know.

The edict did not influence Gilles. He was beyond all rational control. About the middle of August Poitou paid twenty *sous* to have a doublet made for a page who had entered his service. The boy was the son of Eonnet de Villeblanche and his wife Macée. He was assaulted, murdered and incinerated. This was the last recorded murder.

Part Three

PURGATION

15

The Trial

On 24 August 1440 Jean V met his brother, Arthur de Richemont, in Vannes. The object of their discussions was a simple one: to ensure that Charles VII would not attempt to intervene if Gilles' properties in France were attacked and seized. This was hardly likely on the surface. Gilles was no longer called upon to play any part in court or national affairs. He had been conspicuous by his absence in the July campaign against the dissident nobles, the 'Praguerie', which de Richemont had successfully led. As a Marshal of France he should have been present, but he had been ignored. It is doubtful, moreover, whether he had made a very good impression on the Dauphin Louis, who was mean as well as devious. He would not have approved of the extravagance he must have noted during his stay at Tiffauges.

Nonetheless, Jean V had to proceed with caution. He had made the mistake of supporting the rebels, and Charles might take any move against Gilles as a pretext for punitive action. The Duke himself had no authority outside the confines of his own Duchy, but his brother, as Constable of France, had almost unlimited powers of action. It was therefore agreed at Vannes that de Richemont should occupy Tiffauges, liberate Jean Le Ferron who was still held prisoner, and thus deprive Gilles of his last effective stronghold in French territory. In return he would receive certain of Gilles' Breton estates, after they had been legally confiscated, including Bourgneuf-en-Rais.

De Richemont acted immediately. He took Tiffauges without difficulty. When the news reached Machecoul Gilles de Sillé and Robert de Briqueville decided it was time to take to their heels. It is more than probable that over the years, by living off Gilles' generosity and by cheating him in almost every transaction, they had been putting money aside against just such an eventuality. They must have known that the situation could not go on for ever, and now they saw real danger signs. For the Church to make accusations was one thing—the letters patent might be no more than a scrap of paper; but when Jean V and his brother began to move the end was obviously very near.

On September 13 a summons was issued by Jean de Malestroit, in conjunction with the Duke. It repeated much of the material contained in the letters patent but carried the charges one stage further:

> We, not desiring that such crimes and that such an heretical sickness that spreads like a canker unless it is rooted out immediately, should be passed over in silence, by dissimulation or by negligence, moreover, desiring to bring the needful remedies with all speed, by the tenor of these present, we request and require you, you and each of you, without any of you throwing his blame upon another, or excusing himself at the expense of another, by this single binding edict, to cause to appear before us or before our representative in Nantes, on the Monday following the Feast of the Exaltation of the Holy Cross, to whit, the 19th day of September, the said noble Gilles de Rais, knight, our subject and answerable to us in this region. . . .
>
> Given the Tuesday preceding, the 13th Day of September, in the Year of Our Lord 1440.
>
> Thus signed: by command of the said Lord Bishop, Jean Guiolé, who transcribed it.

On the 15th a body of men, under the command of Jean Labbé and accompanied by a lawyer charged to speak in the name of Jean de Malestroit, arrived at Machecoul and demanded that Gilles surrender himself to them. The following warrant was read:

> We, Jean Labbé, captain of arms, acting in the name of my lord Jean V, Duke of Brittany, and Robin Guillaumert, lawyer, acting in the name of Jean de Malestroit, Bishop of Nantes, enjoin Gilles, Comte de Brienne, Lord of Laval, Pouzauges, Tiffauges and other places, Marshal of France and Lieutenant-General of Brittany, to grant us immediate access

to his castle and to constitute himself our prisoner so that he may answer to the triple charge of witchcraft, murder and sodomy.

Gilles surrendered without a struggle. Prelati, Blanchet, Poitou and Henriet were arrested with him. De Sillé and de Briqueville had already fled.

The prisoners were taken to Nantes. Henriet stated later that he was so convinced of the hopelessness of their case that he thought of cutting his throat. On his arrival Gilles was summoned before the civil court, to answer charges of murder and also illegally repossessing Saint-Etienne-de-Mer-Morte. No authenticated record of the proceedings exists, only a later memorandum. Gilles' answers are not given, but the main concern of the hearing seems to have been with the question of property.

Gilles, in fact, was to be subjected to two enquiries and two trials, one secular and one ecclesiastical. Jean de Malestroit, in his capacity both as Bishop and as Chancellor of the Duchy of Brittany, could attack from both sides, so that there was no possibility of Gilles being acquitted. At first Gilles seems not to have realised this. He was still deluded by his own feelings of being above the law.

He was due to appear before the ecclesiastical court on 19 September. On the previous day, Jean de Touscheronde, who had been appointed by the Chief Justice Pierre de l'Hôpital to conduct an enquiry, began hearing evidence. On the 19th Gilles appeared before Jean de Malestroit in the upper room of the castle of La Tour Neuve. The charges were then read to him. Because the charge of heresy was also involved, he was informed that he would be required to answer to Jean Blouyn, who represented the Inquisition in the diocese. Gilles acknowledged the competence of the court and the case was then adjourned until the 28th.

Touscheronde, who was in charge of the secular proceedings, heard further evidence on the 27th, and on the 28th de Malestroit and Jean Blouyn heard ten witnesses in the chapel of the Bishop's palace. Gilles, who had been summoned to be present, did not arrive. On the 28th, 29th, and 30th

Touscheronde continued hearing evidence and took further statements on October 2, 6 and 8.

On the 8th, the witnesses who had given evidence before the secular court appeared before de Malestroit and Blouyn in the lower room of La Tour Neuve. According to the reports, they spoke 'with great cries, and woe, and tears'. The court then moved to the upper room and Gilles appeared. Although the trial was held by the ecclesiastical authorities, the representatives of civil power were there as observers, and the coming together of all concerned marks the beginning of the trial proper. The prosecutor then read the charges. Faced with the body of evidence that had been drawn up against him, Gilles reacted violently, denying the competence of the judges which he had previously recognised. At the preliminary hearing the charges had been nothing like so extensive, or so well substantiated; the major preoccupation had been the affair at Saint-Etienne-de-Mer-Morte. A gentlemen's agreement might still have been arrived at. Now he realised he had no defence whatsoever and that his only hope was to brave it out and deny the competence of the court. His attitude, in view of the gravity of the charges, was dismissed as frivolous. Gilles then denied all the accusations and withdrew all the statements he had previously made, except those concerning his baptism. He then refused to take the oath. He was ordered to take the oath four times, under pain of excommunication. He refused each time. The court then adjourned until the following Tuesday, the 11th, when he was told again that he would be required to take the oath. On the 11th the hearing was further delayed until the 13th and further evidence was taken in the lower room at La Tour Neuve instead. This suggests a certain indecision on the part of the authorities.

On the 13th the public trial began at nine in the morning in the upper room of La Tour Neuve. Most of the local nobility appear to have been present, doubtless anxious to learn the details of what had hitherto only been discussed behind closed doors. It was an intensely dramatic affair. There were moments when the emotion reached such a pitch that the scribe was not able to render the proceedings into the cumbersome impersonality of mediaeval Latin but quoted exchanges directly in the original French. Only the Nuremberg trials, perhaps, can match the horrifying nature of the charges and the intensity of passion they aroused.

First, the formal indictment consisting of forty-nine paragraphs was read. It was, in some ways, a confused document; dates were sometimes inaccurate and the chronology of events inexact. Fifteen paragraphs were concerned with establishing the competence of the court; the remainder contained specific charges. Principal among these were

XV. .... for fourteen years, more or less, every year, every month, every day, every night ... the said Gilles de Rais, possessed by the Evil One, forgetting his salvation, took, killed and cut the throats of many children, boys and girls.

XXVII. Item ... that during the said fourteen years or thereabouts Gilles de Rais, the accused, sometimes at the château of Champtocé, in the diocese of Angers, at Machecoul and Tiffauges, at Vannes, in the house of the said Lemoine, in an upper room of the same house, in the house known as La Suze, situated in the parish of Notre-Dame, to wit in an upper room where he oftentimes retired and passed the night, he killed 140 children or more, boys and girls, in a treacherous, cruel and inhuman fashion ... that the said Gilles de Rais offered the limbs of the said innocents to evil spirits; that both before and after their death, and as they were expiring, he committed the abominable sin of sodomy ... and abused them against nature to satisfy his illicit, carnal and damnable passions, and that afterwards he burned or caused to be burned in these same places the bodies of these innocents, boys and girls, and had the ashes thrown into the cess-pits of the said châteaux....

XXXIV. Item, that during the said fourteen years, more or less, the said Gilles has held discourse with magicians and heretics: that he solicited their aid several times to carry out his purposes; that he communicated and collaborated with them, receiving their dogmas, studied and read books concerning the forbidden arts (alchemy and witchcraft)...

The indictment insists time and time again, in spite of all statements to the contrary, that Gilles' crimes had begun in about 1426. The reason for this may have been political. Jean de Malestroit, who was mainly responsible for drawing up the document, had always been pro-English and had opposed the Duke's frequent alliances with the French. Now, eleven years after the siege of Orléans, he found an opportunity of attributing Gilles' success, like Joan's, to witchcraft and the devil. Even his high honours, Marshal of France and later Lieutenant-General of Brittany, had been obtained by the same trickery. Paragraph XXIV states quite explicitly that, aided by de Sillé, he had employed wizards so that they could 'obtain money for him, reveal hidden treasure, initiate him into other magic arts, obtain honours for him and enable him to take and hold castles and towns...'. Gilles would be condemned and burned just as Joan had been condemned and burned, and the legend of their success would be undermined. De Malestroit's own policies would be vindicated and proved to be in accord with divine will. The verdict would also please Arthur de Richemont, who had been ousted by Gilles' friend and patron, La Trémoille. De Richemont abominated witchcraft in all its forms, as he had shown when he executed Pierre de Giac. Hence the often over-dramatic insistence on fourteen years of crime. As for the alleged number of victims, 140, it is not an unreasonable figure, but can by no means be accepted as definitive.

Asked if he wished to reply to the charges, Gilles answered 'with vanity and arrogance' that he would not, that his judges had no authority over him, that they were 'thieving rogues who took bribes, that he would rather be hanged than answer their questions, and that it was intolerable that he should be brought before them.' The judges then went on to explain, in French, the implications of the indictment, which was, of course, drawn up in Latin, and of the witnesses' testimony. There is no reason to suppose that Gilles had not understood it in Latin the first time, but de Malestroit and Blouyn were evidently concerned that justice should be seen to be done, so that there could be no appeal later, on technical grounds. Gilles still refused to answer and turned to de Malestroit with the following words, which appear in French in the records: 'I will do nothing for you as Bishop of Nantes'. He was then asked again, four times, if he wished to comment or answer questions, on pain of excommunication. He refused, and then addressed himself directly to Pierre de l'Hôpital, stating that he was amazed that the civil authorities could tolerate the proceedings. Pierre de l'Hôpital replied by telling him that he was in contempt of court. Gilles was then formally excommunicated and the decision of the court made public. Gilles appealed, but his appeal was refused on the grounds that it had been made verbally and not in writing. This was a specious argument. They had given him no opportunity to write. They were taking refuge behind a technicality.

It is evident from the report of the proceedings that Gilles' attitude created considerable problems. At first he had seemed quite submissive; he had not resisted arrest. If the trial was to proceed smoothly, as planned, his co-operation was essential. He had to accept the time-table that had been established. If he refused they simply could not proceed. There had been fifteen paragraphs out of forty-nine in the indictment establishing the court's authority, but it was suspect. The members were neither impartial, nor disinterested. Most of them had done business with Gilles, most of them would profit by his downfall. If Gilles persisted in his attitude they might well be in difficulties. They gave him forty-eight hours to reconsider, and reconvened the court for Saturday, October 15.

When Gilles appeared in court two days later he was a changed man. He recognised the competence of the court, admitted the charges in the indictment, except those relating to the invocation of demons, and asked the judges' pardon for the insults and hurtful words he had used. Pardon was granted. The trial could proceed as planned.

As always with Gilles, the crucial moments of his life are shrouded in obscurity. We have no direct knowledge of what happened in the intervening two days. Unquestionably he would have been subjected to considerable pressure. His accusers would automatically present to him the advantages of confession and absolution within the rites of the Church. It was part of their duty which they would have fulfilled with the utmost zeal. The fact that they were at the same time serving their own self-interest by enabling the trial to proceed as planned would not have made their efforts any less sincere. We do not know their methods; we can only say they were successful and that they provided Gilles with the final rôle he was to play in the drama which was his life, that of the perfect penitent.

The court can only have felt relief at Gilles' visible change of heart. Once he had made public confession of his crimes no outside intervention on his behalf would be possible.

Gilles and the Prosecutor took the oath and the first witnesses were called. These were Tiphaine Branchu and Perrine Martin, 'La Meffraye', who had been arrested about the same time as Gilles himself. Unfortunately their testimony has not survived. Prelati was heard on the 16th, Blanchet, Henriet and Poitou on the 17th. Later that same day fifty other witnesses took the oath. On the 19th fifteen witnesses were heard in the upper room of the castle. Gilles had still not spoken or been cross-examined. He seems to have relapsed into his former unco-operative attitude. On the 20th he refused to comment on the evidence that had been so far presented, but agreed to its being published. The Prosecutor then declared that 'to elucidate and scrutinise the truth the more fully the said Gilles should be put to the question'. De Malestroit and Blouyn considered this request, took expert advice and consented.

The following day, at nine in the morning, Gilles was brought to the lower room of La Tour Neuve so that he could be tortured. He asked for a delay of twenty-four hours, during which time 'he would deliberate in such wise on the crimes and offences with which he had been charged that he would content them, and to such a degreee that there would be no need to put him to the question'. He then asked that the Bishop of Saint-Brieuc, representing de Malestroit, Blouyn and Pierre de l'Hôpital, representing the secular authorities, should hear his confession 'outside the place where the torture had been ordered'. It was agreed that he should be given until the second hour of the afternoon so that 'if, by chance, the said Gilles, the accused, confessed the crimes with which he was charged or other similar things, at that time or even later, they would defer the said torture until the following day'.

The court appears to have been unwilling to resort to torture unless it was absolutely necessary, and indeed it was unusual for one of Gilles' rank to be threatened with it. The decision was duly recorded and the presence of several noblemen, especially summoned to witness the proceedings, noted.

A second meeting was held in the lower room at two in the afternoon and the officers of the court sent the Bishop of Saint-Brieuc, Pierre de l'Hôpital, Jean Labbé, Yvon de Rocerf and

Jean de Touscheronde, together with a scribe, to a room in the
tower of La Tour Neuve, where Gilles was lodged, to hear his
statement. Technically speaking, it was outside the official court
proceedings and was distinguished from the second, fuller confession which Gilles made later. It was a dramatic and emotional
session and the record twice breaks into French at moments of
tension.

Gilles admitted his crimes and dated the first murders in 1432.
Asked by Pierre de l'Hôpital where he had learned to commit
such crimes and who had led him to them, he replied 'that he did
them in accordance with his own imagination and thought,
following no man's counsel, but his own, solely for his pleasure
and carnal delight, and with no other end in view'. Pierre de
l'Hôpital found this difficult to accept and again asked him
who had influenced him, and why he had committed the crimes
he had, reminding him that if he made a full confession he
would be more sure of receiving salvation. The following
exchange was then recorded in French.

Gilles :   Alas, my lord, you torment yourself and me with
              you.
l'Hôpital :   I do not torment myself but I am much amazed
              by what you have said and cannot simply be
              content with it. But I would know from you the
              pure truth, for the reasons I have so often put
              to you.
Gilles :   Truly there was no other cause, no other end or
              intention, save what I have told you. I have
              told you greater things than this, and enough
              to hang ten thousand men.

Pierre de l'Hôpital then broke off the examination and sent
for Prelati. It is obvious that he was trying desperately to establish
a connection between the child murders and the invocations.
Possibly this was the only way they could be comprehensible
to him, or he may have felt that the prosecution's case would
be strengthened by reinforcing the witchcraft and heresy
charges. Prelati, in his evidence, confirmed Gilles' statements
concerning the invocations but specifically denied that he had
ever offered the limbs and blood of a child to his familiar,
Barron, although Gilles had provided him with them for that

purpose. L'Hopital then ordered Prelati back to his quarters. Gilles, by now in tears, made this farewell, which again is recorded in French in the record: 'Farewell, François, my friend! Never shall we see each other again in this world; I pray God that He may give you good patience and understanding, for be certain, providing you have good patience and hope in God, we shall see each other in the great joy of Paradise.' He then embraced him and Prelati left the room. One can only surmise his cynical, and unspoken response to this pathetic utterance.

After this, no further mention of torture was made and the following day, October 22, 'at the hour of Vespers', Gilles made a full confession before the whole assembly. It corroborated all that he had said the previous day but filled in many gaps.

*   *   *   *

A week had passed since his humble submission to the court's authority, much of it spent in preparing the long and detailed statement he was to make. Once he had accepted the idea that there was no possibility of acquittal and no hope of salvation here on earth, he was forced to see his life as though it were already over, to see it as something already separate from himself. The time had come to sum up, to make his peace with himself and others before entering the next world, where he would once again be called to account for his actions and to purge his sins. But his fate in that world would depend on the manner of his going from this. Only the Church could provide him with the rituals and practices he needed. True or false, it was the only coherent ideology available: its answers were comprehensive and complete. Without them Gilles could only die in total despair.

As he looked at his life from the distance of impending death he had no doubt where the origin of all his troubles lay. Near the beginning of his confession he told the court 'with great bitterness of heart and much shedding of tears, that he had offended against our Saviour by reason of the fact that he had been poorly controlled in his childhood, when, without check, he had applied himself to everything that might give him pleasure and had taken delight in all illicit acts, and he begged all those present who had children to instruct them in sound doctrines

and to create habits of virtue in their youth and childhood'.
Even allowing for the fact that Gilles knew what ought to be
said, what displays of piety were expected of him, what conventional gestures would be required, this would not account for his
repeated insistence on this point. A few lines later we find that

> he asked that the said confession be published in the vulgar
> tongue [i.e. in French] for all those present, the majority of
> whom had no knowledge of Latin, and that the publication
> and confession of the crimes he had committed be made
> known to them for his shame so that he might the more
> easily obtain the remission of his sins and God's good favour,
> to wipe out the sins he had committed. He said that when
> he was young he had always been delicately nurtured and that
> for his pleasure, and of his own will, he had done all the
> wicked things he could, and that all his endeavour had been
> in illicit and dishonest things he did. He prayed and exhorted
> all mothers and fathers, friends, and all those close to young
> people, to keep them in good habits and to make them
> follow good doctrine and good examples, to instruct them
> in the same and to punish them, lest they fall into the trap
> into which he himself had fallen.

Towards the end of his long recital of crimes, he again
exhorted fathers 'to keep watch over their children, so that
they are not too finely dressed, and not to allow them to live
in idleness, remarking and assuring them that many evils arise
from laziness and excesses at table. . . .'

Despite all arguments to the contrary, despite the frequent
incomprehension of his judges, Gilles insisted at all times that
he had neither been guided nor influenced in his crimes, that
he was totally responsible for the form which they took. He
knew that they sprang from the depths of his personality.

Some writers have assumed that Gilles' comments as to his
having been spoiled refer only to his life with his grandfather.
I can see no reason for this. He uses both the words 'childhood'
and 'youth'. He states, precisely, that the crimes of his youth
were the result of bad training in his childhood. Robert de
Briqueville, who knew Gilles from his earliest years, stated
years after the trial that 'it was necessary to be obedient and
submissive to him, without daring to contradict him or go counter

to his wishes in any way whatsoever'. It is true that de Briqueville was asking for a pardon and would have been anxious to diminish his own degree of responsibility in Gilles' crimes; none the less his statement corroborates what we already know of Gilles' behaviour. It also confirms that the imperiousness and the demand for immediate gratification were there from the first, and bowed to. Now, at the end of his life, Gilles was convinced that in satisfying him and submitting to him almost everyone he had ever known had betrayed him. They had taken him at his word and failed to realise the true import of his message: that he wished to be punished.

In his book *Sexual Deviation* Dr Anthony Storr observes that 'sexual deviations are chiefly the result of the persistence of childhood feelings of guilt and inferiority' and that 'guilt always implies rejection and non-acceptance: and as long as it persists so will any sexual deviation to which it has contributed persist'.

Yet how could Gilles have ever felt rejected or inferior? Few children in history can have been so well endowed, or had such expectations. But expectations of what? Of lands and castles certainly, but how much actual affection did he receive? The sort of affection that would assure a healthy mental life? The truth is that Gilles was less a child than an investment. Too much depended on him; he carried the weight of everyone's hopes and aspirations. He became an object, a function which altered with every person he dealt with. He was a son and heir, a baron, a feudal lord, a clothespeg, a wearer of jewels, a winner of battles, a friend of saints and kings, a patron of the arts, a dispenser of benefices, a source of shelter, food and profit. And while he performed and glittered, inside he felt miserable, lonely, rejected and guilty, and no one recognised the fact; no one was concerned with his human needs. Being everyone's object, he never experienced himself as subject, as a person in his own right.

Freud has pointed out that guilt-feelings need not necessarily be attached to any specific incident or misdemeanour. A feeling of guilt is a general state and often *precedes* punishable action. When a child is naughty he may be so in order to be punished. This may be the means of alleviating intolerable feelings that have been mounting up inside and which can be discharged, for the time being at least, when he is chastised. Gilles' complaint, and it was a justifiable one, was that he had never received this correction and consequently had never known this discharge of emotion. He was left with this intolerable burden inside him. Anyone who has seen a child in a tantrum will have recognised the moment when the situation goes out of control and when the child becomes terrified by the emotional forces it has unleashed. It seems literally possessed, swept away by its own feelings, and its cries change from being cries of anger and frustration to cries of distress, to a demand to be rescued by some more responsible person; by, in fact, an adult. What can a child who is not rescued from this plight conclude, except that he is not worth bothering about, that he does not merit a few moments of someone's real attention, that he is worthless? Gilles understood that punishment, properly applied, can be as much an expression of loving concern as a cuddle or a kiss, and that in a sense it was his right. But no such concern had ever been shown him. He therefore concluded that he had never been loved and, worse, that there was nothing in him that was worth loving.

It was Gilles' misfortune that circumstances both in his family and in his society conspired to aggravate his condition. The arrival of his brother René could only have increased his feelings of unease, and when his parents died in 1415 it must have seemed like the final rejection. By the time he was eleven his worst feelings about himself had been confirmed.

Something might still have been done had he not fallen into the hands of his grandfather. His criminal attitudes provided Gilles with the kind of superficial excitement and sensation which on the one hand acted as a partial release but on the other obscured his deepest needs. For years he and his grandfather were able to give free rein to their violence and banditry. The society in which they lived was too unstable and corrupt to apply any kind of corrective. As Gilles grew up his importance increased; he was out of the reach of the law. Moreover his society needed him, it needed his money and his troops. His peers tolerated what they could not prevent, but tried at the same time to exploit him. If Gilles remained all his life a violent, aggressive, spoiled child his society had a vested interest in keeping him so. It was what made him a good soldier and, until 1433 at least, good soldiers were needed. Thus Gilles found himself praised and honoured for those very acts which, in part at least, were intended as provocations.

Gilles' response had been to multiply his crimes, like a gambler increasing the stakes. Continually he went to the brink, continually he invited ruin.

With the execution of Joan and the death of his grandfather he had again experienced feelings of extreme rejection, and under the pressure of circumstances, having no means of releasing the tension, what had once seemed aggression revealed its true nature as self-hate. But for him to have given real expression to this hate he would have to have killed himself. What he did was to kill himself over and over again, symbolically through the victims that were brought to him. Or rather he killed the rejected part of himself. There was still the other, the acceptable part of himself, symbolised in the choir-boys of his chapel, his 'little angels' whom he pampered and spoiled. The contrast in his treatment of the two groups perfectly expressed the conflict in his mind. So, too, did the ritual pattern which the murders took: the initial attack, followed by cuddling and fondling and reassurance, ending with sexual assault and death. It is difficult not to see here, graphically presented, Gilles' own childhood as he had experienced it, with all its conflicting emotions and impressions.

The crimes were repeated remorselessly but they evoked no response. Not merely that, they provided no genuine resolution of the conflict, only temporary relief. Hence the increasing depression and the appeals to religion, the displays of public piety. When this failed there was the final, and successful, provocation at Saint-Etienne-de-Mer-Morte.

At the beginning of the trial Gilles had gone through all his normal motions; he had stamped and raged and defied like an arrogant uncontrollable child. Once he had accepted the idea that punishment was certain and inescapable, he achieved a state of calm which was to be with him to the end.

Gilles had known similar security of mind once before in his adult life, during the months he spent with Joan, and his relationship with her displays many of the same features as his new-found relationship with the Church. As well as supplying friendship, Joan had imposed rigorous standards of conduct, which he had accepted. For once he sacrificed his own immediate pleasure to a greater purpose. In her own down-to-earth way Joan was no less exacting than Rome. She was, moreover, sexually an ambiguous figure: a woman who dressed and behaved as a man. As such she represented no sexual threat but was able to fill a number of rôles as required, male or female, mother, father, sister, brother, friend, and, whatever her function, she could be regarded as an ideal, to be loved, respected and admired.

The Church, as a body, exhibits the same ambiguity, for it is a mother composed almost entirely of men. As such it is able to perform a dual rôle, alternating gentle feminine concern with severe masculine control. Gilles had found the perfect parent at last.

* * * *

On October 23, the secular court heard the confessions of Poitou and Henriet, which were identical in almost every detail with the ones they had made before the ecclesiastical court. Both were condemned to death.

On the 25th in the upper room of La Tour Neuve, Gilles also was condemned to death, having been found guilty of 'perfidious, heretical apostasy and the invocation of demons' as well as the unnatural vice of sodomy with children. He was then formally excommunicated and immediately readmitted to the church. He asked to be allowed to make confession. His request was granted and a Carmelite monk, Jean Jouvenel, was appointed. He was then transferred to the castle of Bouffay, to appear before the secular court which had to settle the affair of Saint-Etienne-de-Mer-Morte. Pierre de l'Hôpital confirmed the fine of 50,000 *écus* already imposed. The sum was to be raised from the sale of goods and lands. For his other crimes he was to be hanged and burned. The date and time of the execution were fixed for eleven o'clock on the following day. Poitou and Henriet were to be executed with him. Gilles asked that he should be executed first, so that he might set them a good example, seeing that it was he who had first led them into crime, and also so that they should not suspect that, while they were to be killed, he himself would escape.

In view of his contrite attitude, the court decreed that Gilles' body be taken from the flames before it was burst open by the heat and gave permission for it to be buried in a church of his own choice. He asked to be interred in the church of the monastery of Notre-Dame des Carmes in Nantes. He also requested that the Bishop of Nantes and his clergy should walk in solemn procession to the place of execution so that he and his servants might be kept in a firm hope of salvation. This too was agreed.

The following day, October 26, at about nine o'clock, the procession began. It was impressive and moving, with all the splendour of ritual and music that the church could offer. It was yet more theatre. Gilles himself was a model of piety, encouraging Poitou and Henriet, exhorting them to think of the salvation of their souls. He also prayed to Saint James and also, significantly, in view of his association with Joan, to Saint Michael.

He maintained his firm resolution to the end. As the fire was lit he was hanged. Shortly after he expired his body was removed from the flames and laid out by four noble ladies of the town. He was pampered and privileged to the end. Poitou and Henriet were shown no such consideration; they were burned to a cinder and their ashes scattered.

Prelati, who was condemned to perpetual imprisonment, managed to escape, but only to be hanged later for further crimes. Blanchet was fined 300 *écus* and banished for life. Perrine Martin, 'La Meffraye', hanged herself in her cell.

16

Bluebeard

Within a short space of time Gilles passed into legend. His story became mingled with that of Bluebeard and it is by that name that he has been almost universally known, even in the works of a rationalist like Bernard Shaw. It is an indication of the impact which his case made upon his time that he should be transformed into a legendary figure like Faust and Don Juan. Perhaps it was the only way in which the local populace could cope with so horrendous a career. As the myth developed, the sadistic homesexual elements disappeared, to be replaced by stories of abducted girls and murdered wives.

Yet fragments of history survived. In his basic study of Gilles' life, the Abbé Bossard quotes two versions of his story taken from the *Larousse of the Nineteenth Century*. One of them was a Breton song with stanzas alternating between an Old Man and a group of Young Girls.

Old Man: 'Young women of Pléeur, why are you silent? Why do you no longer go to feasts and to dancing?'

Young Girls: 'Ask us why the nightingale is silent in the wood and the finches no longer make sweet song.'

O.M.: 'Forgive me, young maids, but I am a stranger: I have come from afar ... and I do not know the reason for the sadness that I see written on your faces.'

Y.G.: 'We weep for Gwenola, the most beautiful and most beloved of us all.'

O.M.: 'What became of Gwenola? Young maids, you are silent. What is happening here?'

Y.G.: 'Alas! Alas! the wicked Bluebeard has slain the gentle Gwenola, as he has killed all his wives!'

O.M.: (In terror) 'Bluebeard lives here! Ah! Fly quickly, my children. The ravening wolf is not more terrible than the wild Baron; the bear is more gentle than the accursed Baron de Rais.'

Y.G.: 'We are not able to fly: we are bound to the Barony of Rais, and we belong, body and soul, to my lord Bluebeard.'

O.M.: 'I will deliver you, for I am Jean de Malestroit, Bishop of Nantes, and I have sworn to defend my flock.'

Y.G.: 'Gilles de Laval does not believe in God!'

O.M.: 'He shall come to a bad end! I swear it by the living God!'

Two important memories persist in this version; first the rôle of Jean de Malestroit; second the hopeless situation in which the local population found itself, bound by feudal ties to their brutal overlord.

A further legend survives:

Tired of making war against the English, Messire Gilles de Laval had retired to his castle de Rais, between Elven and Questembert. All his time was spent in joy, feasting and pleasure. One day a knight, Count Odon de Tréméac, lord of Krevent and other places, rode by his castle on his way to Morlaix; at his side rode a beautiful young woman, his betrothed, Blanche de l'Herminière. Gilles de Rais invited them both to rest awhile and emptied a cup of hippocras with them. But the travellers were anxious to be on their way. But Gilles de Rais was so pressing and above all so friendly that evening came without their giving a thought to their departure.

Suddenly at a sign from their master, archers seized Count Odon de Tréméac and threw him into a deep dungeon: then Gilles spoke to the young girl of marriage. Blanche shed many tears while the chapel was lit by a thousand candles, the bell rang joyously and everything was made ready for the ceremony. Blanche was led to the altar: she was as pale as a lovely lily and she was trembling. My lord de Laval, superbly dressed with a magnificent red beard, came and stood at her side.

'Quick, master Chaplain, marry us.'

'I do not want my lord for my husband,' cried Blanche de l'Herminière.

'And I wish us to be married.'

'Do not do it, sir priest,' the young woman said, sobbing.

'Obey. I order you.'

Then, as Blanche tried to fly, Gilles seized her in his arms. 'I will give you my castles, my woods, my meadows, my fields.'

'Let me go.'

'I give myself to you, body and soul!'

'I accept! I accept! Do you hear me, Gilles de Rais? I accept and henceforth you belong to me.' Blanche had just been transformed into a blue devil, who now stood at the Baron's side.

'Curses,' cried Gilles.

'Gilles de Laval,' said the demon with a sinister laugh, 'God has grown tired of your sins; now you belong to the powers of hell and from this day forward you shall wear their livery.' At the same time he made a sign and the beard of Gilles de Laval changed from the red it had been to the darkest hue. 'That is not all,' the demon continued, 'in the future you will no longer be Gilles de Laval, you will be Bluebeard, the most terrifying of men, a bogey-man for little children. Your name will be accursed for all eternity and your ashes, after your death, will be scattered to the winds, while your wicked soul will go down into the depths of hell.'

Gilles cried that he repented. The devil spoke to him of his many victims, of his seven wives, whose bodies had been cast into the castle cellars.' He added, 'The Count Odon de Tréméac, whom I accompanied here in the form of Blanche de l'Herminière, is riding this very moment on the road from Elven in company with all the gentlemen from Redon.'

'What are they coming for?'

'To avenge the deaths of all those you have killed.'

'Then I am lost?'

'No, not yet, for your hour has not struck.'

'Who will stop them?'

'I will, for I have need of your help and your aid, my good knight.'

'Would you do that?'

'I shall do it, for you will serve me a thousand times better living than dead. And now farewell, Gilles de Rais, and remember that you belong to me, body and soul.'

And the devil disappeared in a cloud of sulphur. He kept his word and kept the gentlemen from Redon from entering. But from that moment on Gilles was only known in that part of the land as the man with the blue beard.

Local memories were more accurate. Rural France changed little either in its way of life or methods of agriculture between the mid-fifteenth and the mid-nineteenth century, so that when the Abbé Bossard began collecting material for his book he found a strong oral tradition. As he travelled round, wherever Gilles had once owned a castle people would point to it and say, 'That was Bluebeard's castle.' One incident he relates is worth quoting:

One day, while walking through the ruins of the castle [Tiffauges], we met . . . a group of tourists sitting on the grass near the base of the great tower: in their midst was an old woman from the locality who was talking about Bluebeard. This woman is still alive: she was born within the immediate vicinity of the fortress and her family lived there for 300 years, up until about 1850.

To get her to talk more freely the Abbé and his companion adopted a somewhat superior and incredulous attitude, asking her many questions,

but nothing could shake her belief: Bluebeard had been the master of this castle: her parents had always told her so, on the faith of their own forebears.

'Look,' she added suddenly, 'come with me and I'll take you to the very room where he used to cut the little children's throats.' She led us to the main tower and pointed to a small door, high up, in the angle of two immense walls. 'That's the room,' she said.

'But tell us once more, who told you so?'

'My old parents always told me and they knew it well enough. In the old days there was a staircase leading up to it and I often went up when I was young. Now the staircase has crumbled away, and they say, the room itself is almost full of debris where the roof has fallen in.'

The Abbé made his way up to the room with some difficulty. There he found, well preserved, the immense fireplace in which so many bodies had been burned.

Appendix

CHRONOLOGICAL LIST OF KNOWN VICTIMS
(First names are given where they are known)

1432–3
Jean Jeudon, aged 12.
Jean Roussin, aged 9.
Edelin, aged 8.
Chastelier.
Sorin? (Evidence confused).

1437
Thierry.

1438
February–March: Guillaume Delit.
June 16: Jenvret, aged 9.
June 24: Jean Degrepie.
June 26: Jean Hubert, 14.
August: Fougère, aged 12.
September: Loessart, aged 10.
      Bernard, aged 12.
October: Perrot Degaye, aged 10.
Oran.

1439
April 12: Bouer, aged 8.
May: Sergent, aged 8.
June 29: Olivier Darel, aged 7 or 8.
August: Colin Avril.
August 25: Bernard le Camus, aged 15.
August 28: Jean Toutblanc, aged 13.
Two sons of Robin Pavot, both aged about 8.
Two sons of Eustache Drouet, aged 7 and 10.
Two sons of Guillaume Hamelin, aged 7 and 15.

1440

Unknown boy aged 15 or 16.
Unknown boy.
Unknown boy, nephew of Jean de Lanté.
March: Thouars, aged 12.
March: Guillaume le Barbier, aged 16.
April–May: Kerguen, aged 15.
       Aisé, aged 10.
June 24: Jamet Brice, aged 8 or 9.
July: Lavary, aged 10.
Mid-August: de Villeblanche.

Chronological Table

1400	Jeanne Chabot makes Guy de Laval her heir, on condition he takes the name de Rais.
1402	Jeanne Chabot disinherits Guy de Laval and makes a will in favour of Catherine de Machecoul.
1404	Marriage of Guy de Laval/Rais and Marie de Craon, daughter of Catherine de Machecoul and Jean de Craon. Birth of Gilles de Rais.
1406	Jeanne Chabot dies.
1407 November 23	René de la Suze, Gilles' brother, born.
1415	Marie de Rais, Gilles' mother, dies.
September 28	Guy de Rais dies.
October 25	Amaury de Craon, heir of Jean de Craon, killed at the battle of Agincourt. Gilles inherits the Craon estates and fortune.
1420 February	Jean de Craon marries Catherine's grandmother, Anne de Sillé.
November 22	Gilles kidnaps his cousin Catherine de Thouars and marries her.
1427	Gilles' first experience of campaigning under the protection of Ambroise de Loré.
1429 April 8	After Joan of Arc's arrival at court (March 6) Gilles signs a contract binding him to Georges de la Trémoille.
April-May-June	The liberation of Orléans and subsequent campaign.
July 17	Gilles named Marshal of France on the day of Charles' coronation.

September 8	Marie de Rais, Gilles' daughter, born.
1430	Private campaigns against Jean de Bueil and La Trémoille's political enemies.
December	Gilles at Louviers, within reach of Joan, who had been taken prisoner.
1432	Gilles participates in the battle at Lagny.
November 15	Jean de Craon dies. His will indicates an estrangement from his grandson.
1434	
March	Gilles' first sexual crimes. Gilles present at Sillé-le-Guillaume among the royal troops. No battle takes place. Creates his chapel. Is nominated Canon of Saint-Hilaire de Poitiers. Receives money to fight against the Duke of Burgundy but sends his brother René instead.
Autumn	Takes up residence in Orléans.
1435	Gilles raises money to pay for La Trémoille's expedition. Does not complete the transaction.
May	Pays for the production of the 'Mistère du Siège d'Orléans'. Liquidation of his fortune.
July 2	Gilles' family obtain an injunction against him, forbidding further sales of family property.
September	Guillaume de la Jumelière leaves Gilles' service.
1437	René de la Suze siezes the castle of Champtocé.
November	Jean V de Bretagne makes Gilles Lieutenant-General.
November 12	Gilles borrows money from Jean V with Champtocé as security. Stages a false attack on Champtocé with the connivance of his brother. Interest in alchemy grows.
1438	Children's bodies removed from Champtocé.
1439	Gilles sends Blanchet to Italy to look for alchemists.
May	Prelati is brought to Tiffauges by Blanchet.
November	Blanchet takes fright and flees.
December	The Dauphin visits Tiffauges. All alchemical apparatus is destroyed.

1440

May	Violent entry into the church of Saint-Etienne-de-Mer-Morte.
July	Gilles meets Jean V at Josselin. Jean de Malestroit begins investigation into Gilles' crimes.
September 15	Gilles arrested.
September 19	First sitting of the court at Nantes.
October 13	Gilles excommunicated. He refuses to accept the competence of the court.
October 15	Gilles submits to his judges and recognises the competence of the court.
October 21	Gilles begins his confession.
October 23	Henriet and Poitou sentenced to death.
October 25	Gilles sentenced to death.
October 26	Execution of Gilles, Henriet and Poitou.

Index